W9-AVN-898

Praise for *Prince Charming Isn't Coming*

"Insightful analysis of why women are often money-phobic, plus a practical plan for change."
—*Mademoiselle*

"Her down-to-earth book offers readers a practical, seven-step guide to overcoming this negative—and dangerous—attitude and, in the process, gaining the bonus of far greater self-esteem."
—*New York Newsday*

"Stanny's book is part motivator and part primer, recounting tales of women who dove into the investment world and surfaced feeling self-assured." —*The Kansas City Star*

"*Prince Charming Isn't Coming* is a book every woman must read. It addresses the taboo of women understanding the nature of their relationship to money in a totally readable, wise, and immensely helpful way. I think it's breakthrough and I'm very glad I read it."

—Judith Krantz

"Barbara Stanny writes from the heart. When it comes to learning about money, she's been there, done that, and lived to tell about it. Her book is as much a personal financial odyssey as it is a guide to the world of successful money management. A genuinely good read."

—Esther M. Berger, CFP, author of *Money Smart: Secrets Women Need to Know about Money* and *MoneySmart Divorce*

"Stanny combines information with inspiration. Any woman who is serious about money needs this book."

—Victoria Felton-Collins, Ph.D., CFP, author of *Couples and Money*

"*Prince Charming Isn't Coming* is 'must' reading for every woman who wants to take control over her own financial destiny. It removes fear and intimidation and replaces them with confidence and motivation. A great book!"

—Ginger Applegarth, CFP, CLU, ChFC, author of *The Money Diet*

Barbara Stanny is a journalist and former syndicated columnist and career counselor. She is the coauthor of two books, including *How to Be Happily Employed*. She holds a master's degree in counseling psychology and lives in Port Townsend, Washington, with her family.

Barbara Stanny

PRINCE CHARMING ISN'T COMING

How Women Get Smart About Money

PENGUIN BOOKS

PENGUIN BOOKS

Published by the Penguin Group
Penguin Putnam Inc., 375 Hudson Street,
New York, New York 10014, U.S.A.
Penguin Books Ltd, 27 Wrights Lane,
London W8 5TZ, England
Penguin Books Australia Ltd,
Ringwood, Victoria, Australia
Penguin Books Canada Ltd, 10 Alcorn Avenue,
Toronto, Ontario, Canada M4V 3B2
Penguin Books (N.Z.) Ltd, 182–190 Wairau Road,
Auckland 10, New Zealand
Penguin Books India, 210 Chiranjiv Tower, 43 Nehru Place,
New Delhi 11009, India

Penguin Books Ltd, Registered Offices:
Harmondsworth, Middlesex, England

First published in the United States of America by Viking Penguin,
a member of Penguin Putnam Inc. 1997
Published in Penguin Books 1999

10 9 8 7 6 5

The individual experiences recounted in this book are true. However, in some instances, names and descriptive details have been changed to protect the privacy of the people involved.

PUBLISHER'S NOTE
This publication is designed to provide accurate and authoritative information with regard to the subject matter covered. It is sold with the understanding that the publisher is not engaged in rendering financial, accounting, or other professional service. If financial advice or other expert assistance is required, the service of a competent professional person should be sought.

THE LIBRARY OF CONGRESS HAS CATALOGUED THE HARDCOVER AS FOLLOWS:
Stanny, Barbara.
Prince Charming isn't coming: how women get smart about money / Barbara Stanny.
p. cm.
ISBN 0-670-86689-X (hc.)
ISBN 0 14 02.6693 3 (pbk.)
1. Women—Finance, Personal. I. Title.
HG179.S795 1997
332.024'042—dc21   97–12681

Printed in the United States of America
Set in ITC Century Light
Designed by Kathryn Parise

To my girls, Melissa, Julie, and Anna.

And to my husband, Cal.

Acknowledgments

• •

If anyone had told me, years ago, I'd write a book about money, I would have considered them crazy. And in truth, the fact that I did write such a book is nothing short of a miracle. But this "miracle" could not have happened without the help and encouragement of so many wonderful people. Writing this book was a labor of love, and in many ways, a team effort. To everyone on my team, a personal thank you.

To Laurel Cook, who nudged me over my writer's block by gently suggesting I pretend I'm writing her a letter. The first two chapters began as letters to Laurel;

To Carol Adrienne, a dear friend who deftly guided me through the proposal and very first draft with unbridled enthusiasm;

To Doris Ober, who was right there, every page of the way, with her skillful editing, astute comments, and indispensable encouragement;

To Theo Gund, who believed in this project with such intensity, I can never thank her enough;

To Candice Fuhrman, a superb agent (and delightful person) who made it happen;

To Mindy Werner and Beena Kamlani, my editors at Viking, who were so professional, so right-on and such fun to work with, I am a bit sad the writing is done;

To Tracy Gary, a remarkable role model, tireless mentor, and genuinely supportive friend, whose impact on me personally made this book possible;

To my parents, Richard and Annette Bloch, who lovingly and enthusiastically support me, even after they read the first chapter;

To Cal, who not only gave me the benefit of his wisdom and expertise, but also kept me balanced throughout the process;

And to all the women I interviewed, who were amazingly generous with their time and surprisingly candid about a subject rarely discussed so openly. These women were my teachers. To them I am forever indebted.

Contents

● ●

"*The time for women to embrace their power . . . has at long last arrived. If you are a woman, you need to know this is not the time to hold back; it is a time to go for it.*"
—Patricia Aburdene, *Megatrends for Women*

"*From the heart, may it go to the heart.*"
—Beethoven, on the completion of one of his symphonies

Introduction

••••••••••••••••••••••••••••

I grew up believing that one day my prince would come. He would whisk me off my feet and we'd fly blissfully into the sunset. I spent much of my life searching for this prince. Several times I thought I had found him. Each time I was wrong. But I kept looking. I kept waiting. Then one day, as if jolted awake from a deep sleep, I realized that Prince Charming wasn't coming. The realization hit me with the force of a tidal wave, and I knew my life would never be the same again.

That was the day I shifted my focus from "out there" and began to take a long, hard look at myself. What I saw was life-changing. I discovered that I had wings. These wings had been with me since the day I was born, but somewhere along the way, I learned that a prince wouldn't be attracted to a woman who could fly. Afraid and discouraged, I tucked my wings away, and they shriveled from disuse. Eventually I forgot they'd ever existed. But suddenly, on that day of awakening, I felt their presence again—the little flutters, the tiny surge of power. I knew that with a bit of effort, I could soar like a bird, go wherever I wanted to go, accomplish what I'd never believed was possible.

I have since come to realize something else. I am not alone. Each of us was born with wings. Each of us has the ability to go farther than we ever thought possible, to do things beyond our wildest imaginings. Prince Charming Isn't Coming is meant to be about far more than money. It is about waking up, reclaiming our power, remembering we can fly.

• • •

When I first started toying with the idea for this book, I called an author friend of mine. "I want to write about how women go from feeling stupid to acting smart about money," I said. "What do you think?"

"Great idea," she replied enthusiastically.

A few days later, I got a note from her. After reading it, I understood why I was compelled to write this book.

"I really liked your idea," my friend wrote, "but I was totally exempting myself from your story of being able to go from 'stupid' to smart about money. It was for other women, not me." Then what she was saying to herself dawned on her. "It was quite a jolt to me to see how stone closed I was. Probably a first step to thinking, Maybe . . ."

That's the only thought you need to hold as you turn the pages of this book. "Maybe—just maybe—I can become smart with money." Or, "Maybe I could be *even smarter.*" Getting smart about money is a lifelong process. It doesn't matter where you are now: just beginning or somewhat seasoned. Getting smart with money is *not* something only other people do. *You* can do it too.

Admittedly, there was a time when I felt exactly like my friend. In fact, for most my adult life, I truly believed that managing money was a man's job, that men were privy to secrets I would never know. Sure, there were women who were smart with money, but they were "different" than me. I thought you were either born with money smarts or you weren't. Obviously, I wasn't. So I waited for Prince Charming to take up the slack.

But that was before I interviewed scores of women who had become financially savvy, before I finally understood what I needed to do, before my own bungling attempts to achieve financial autonomy actually bore fruit.

Today I am convinced beyond a shadow of a doubt: *There is no reason in the world why any woman can't be proficient in managing money.* Granted, men, by and large, *are* more likely to handle finances, not because they are any more capable, but because, like it or not, they have been groomed for the job.

"I see no difference in the ability of men and women to handle money," professes financial writer Jane Bryant Quinn. "It's just that men get more experience because they have had to deal with it even if they hate it."

Terry Savage, author of *Terry Savage's New Money Strategies for the 90's*, agrees. "It's what you grow up with," she explains. "If you sent a man to a mall and told him, 'I want one Estée Lauder lipstick, one Clinique blusher, and some Wamsutta sheets if they are on sale,' he wouldn't know where to start. Well, when I say to you, 'We need a mutual fund, a money market account, and we also need to check into some disability insurance,' it's the same thing. Our eyes glaze over. That's what we do as women. 'I don't know about disability. Where do I get that?' The truth is it's familiarity."

The time has come to groom ourselves, to become familiar with the financial side of life. We must give money management the same priority, the same level of attention, and the same kind of matter-of-factness that we give our personal grooming, our homes, our job responsibilities, and our health care. (How many of us read the nutritional label on a box of cereal more mindfully than our financial statements? And find the label easier to understand?)

This book is written with one purpose in mind—to urge you to accept financial responsibility as simply another part of life; to renounce the Prince and become personally accountable. Indeed, something wonderful happens when we stop searching for Prince Charming and start relying on ourselves.

Prince Charming, in truth, is nothing more than a projection of our disowned selves. He rose out of the ashes of our perceived incompetence, out of our lack of self-trust. He is the self we refuse to see. So often we feel inadequate, or as one woman put it, "like there is something intrinsically wrong with me." We deny our potential power, projecting it onto a person or a thing, real or imagined, which becomes the Prince who will save us. When we finally do recognize the "Prince" inside ourselves, we discover we have access to all those princely qualities we thought we lacked.

Through the stories told in this book, you will learn how I and so many women have discovered the "prince" within, have found our *own* way to financial enlightenment, and how you can too. In the following pages, you will:

- meet role models, learn firsthand how they became smart;
- understand the underlying factors that have prevented you from financial mastery;
- demystify money and debunk the myths that may have kept you stuck;
- discover specific steps for getting smart with money, which deal not only with technical skills but also with psychological obstacles.

One word of caution: What you are about to read in this book will *not* help you get out of debt, deal with creditors, improve bad spending habits, or meet monthly expenses (although Chapter Three concludes with some ideas and resources for overcoming excess spending and debt). Once you resolve these crucial issues, however, *Prince Charming Isn't Coming* will show you how to wisely manage your money, protect your future, and empower yourself personally.

Prince Charming Isn't Coming is divided into three parts. Part One, The Problem, presents my personal story and how I was motivated to take charge of my financial life; the specific issues women face; why it's so important to become financially enlightened; and what it means to be money smart. Part Two, The Process, distills what I have learned, from both my experiences and my interviews, into a series of insights necessary for getting smart with money. Each chapter in this part (and Part Three) concludes with a "Recap" of the chapter's message and offers specific suggestions, in the form of a to-do list, for a course of action aimed at achieving results. If you follow these suggestions, you will find yourself painlessly on your way to becoming financially responsible and economically independent.

Finally, Part Three, The Power, explores a profound and compelling truth: Financial responsibility will give you far more than a bigger bank balance. Financial clarity brings a freedom and peace of mind that no amount of money could ever buy. Furthermore, when freedom is combined with responsibility, an economically independent woman can become a powerful force in the world.

The Most Important Messages of All

There are two vital messages I hope to convey throughout this book. They will make all the difference in your ability to assume financial control and the ease with which you will accomplish it. I call these the *fundamental truths for taking financial responsibility*. If you take these two truths to heart, you will avoid so much of the pain and frustration, the lost time and tragic consequences, that women often suffer when they deal with their money.

Fundamental Truth #1: You don't need a lot of money to begin.

So many women I meet fool themselves into thinking that if they don't have a lot of money, there is not much they can do. That is simply not true. I've talked to teachers, bookkeepers, secretaries, people whose incomes were fairly low on the pay scale, yet over time, they had built sizable net worths. Indeed, the women you will meet in this book run the gamut on the economic scale. Some are quite wealthy. The majority, however, have moderate means. Yet regardless of their cash flow, they became savvy investors.

This is the most exciting—and probably least understood—part about financial success: You can start with very little money, as little as $25 to $50. Anyone can create wealth without a big wad of cash.

Anne Scheiber is a wonderful example. Anne, a government worker who never earned more than $4,000 a year, quit her job in 1944 with a total of $5,000 in savings. She promptly invested her nest egg in the stock market, and she kept a close watch on her account. "Over the next half century," an article in the *San Francisco Chronicle* reported, "Scheiber parlayed that $5,000 into a portfolio . . . worth about $22 million by the time she died." (Incidentally, what made her story newsworthy was not just her wealth but what she did with it, as I discuss in later chapters.)

Anne Scheiber's story is admittedly exceptional. But our results don't have to be so dramatic to be successful. And we certainly don't need $5,000 to start.

An accountant, for example, told me that she was making only $15,000 a year in her first job. Still she managed to put $50 into her mutual funds almost every month for several years. As her salary increased, so did her contributions. "The funds weren't real risky," she explained. "They were very conservative, but they've done very well." Well enough so that eventually she purchased a house with her profits.

But what if coming up with an extra $50 seems impossible? Countless women I meet exclude themselves from investing because they genuinely believe they haven't enough. I remember attending a financial seminar once when a woman asked: "I hardly make any money. What if I don't have *anything* to invest?" Phyllis Helfand, a stockbroker who was leading the seminar, didn't miss a beat. "Try this," she replied. "If you skipped, let's say, one caffè latte every day and put that money in a jar, at the end of the year you'd have $630, or $52.50 a month." Phyllis was not suggesting a life of self-denial. Whether or not we drink coffee, if we simply put $1.75 aside every day, we'd have over $50 a month to put in savings. Most of us squander at least that much on frivolous items all the time.

If we kept adding $630 to the jar every year, Phyllis continued, twenty-five years later we'd have $15,750. Not bad. But, Phyllis emphasized, if we had put that same amount in an investment that earned 10 percent (which is the average annual return for stocks), "at the end of twenty-five years we'd be looking at $61,958." That's a big difference.

We'll be talking at length about investing throughout the book. Even if you have no extra cash, not even a few dollars left over at the end of the month, don't exempt yourself from this endeavor. You, or your spouse, have a retirement plan at work. (If you don't, you should!) Studies consistently show that most retirement programs, including IRAs, are underfunded or poorly managed, and women, in particular, are too conservatively invested. Tragically, most people are unaware of the problem until it's too late. Which brings us to the second fundamental truth.

Fundamental Truth #2: Don't wait until a crisis to get started.

Too many women, myself included, wait until we're in dire straits before we do anything. I saw this over and over again in the women I interviewed.

"It was out of desperation that I finally recognized I had to do something," said a recent widow whose husband had secretly taken out so many loans on his insurance policy that there was nothing left for her.

A crisis, by definition, is a quick and sudden change marked by instability and chaos. Put another way, a crisis is an event that feels as if the gods are trying to shake us into action. And sadly, it often does take a crisis to wake us up and get us moving—anything from divorce or the death of a spouse to a staggering tax bill or a winning lottery ticket. (Yes, even windfalls create crises.)

But is that the only way? Must we wait for a crisis or a sudden shock to wake us up? The answer is an emphatic *no*. All it takes is a decision. A simple decision, a declarative sentence, "I can do that and I *will* do that," can be the switch that starts the process rolling. It's immeasurably preferable to a catastrophe. A crisis is the worst time to initiate anything. We simply can't think straight. We tend to make terrible decisions, sink into paralysis, and leave ourselves wide open to financial losses. But as a Chinese sage once advised, any crisis can be avoided if we "deal with the big while it is still small."

Imagine what our life would be like if we didn't wait for a crisis but made a conscious choice to become smart about money. We can take our lead from women whose determination rather than a disaster was the catalyst for change. One young woman, for example, described watching her boss make a fortune in the stock market. "I decided if she could do that, I could too," she told me. Or a mother, whose own mother was also financially inept, explained her motivation: "I feel a tremendous responsibility to my children, like I'm pioneering the way for them." Then there were all those women who realized, as one did, "My husband didn't know a thing about money and didn't care, so I figured it was up to me." Or another, who admitted, "I'd never learn about investing for its own sake, but I am very clear. I want my money to last. I want to live on it. So it has to grow beyond inflation." These women allowed potentially negative situations to spur them into action.

The writer Thomas Carlyle once said: "The best effect of any book is that it excites the reader to self-activity." It would be wonderful if this book (rather than a crisis) excited every one of its readers to action. For some, however, the first steps are the toughest part. Yet invariably the first step is the most empowering. I am reminded of something the poet Guillaume Apollinaire wrote:

> *Come to the edge, he said*
> *They said: we are afraid*
> *Come to the edge, he said*
> *They came*
> *He pushed them . . . And they flew.*

My hope is that the stories you read throughout the book will be compelling enough to draw you to the edge, inspiring enough to give you whatever push you need, persuasive enough to prove that your only safety is in taking charge of your future, and illuminating enough so you can indeed discover the awesome freedom of financial autonomy. If you have any doubts, at least be open to the possibility that maybe, just maybe, you can actually do it . . . maybe, just maybe, you too can fly.

• • •

Before We Begin . . .

Let's shift the focus to you and your situation. Below is a questionnaire: "Where Are You When It Comes to Money?" Take a moment to fill it out.

Where Are You When It Comes to Money?

• • • • • • • • • • • • • • • •

Respond to the following statements by circling the number that most clearly reflects your feelings: 1=*never;* 2=*sometimes;* 3=*always.*

1. I am comfortable talking about money and my finances.		1 - 2 - 3
2. I feel excited about managing my own money.		1 - 2 - 3
3. I feel good about the way I budget my money.		1 - 2 - 3
4. I feel knowledgeable about the various investment options.		1 - 2 - 3
5. I feel competent about investing in the market.		1 - 2 - 3
6. I feel secure knowing I have adequate savings.		1 - 2 - 3
7. I feel that no matter what happens, I can take care of myself financially.		1 - 2 - 3
8. I pay my bills on time.		1 - 2 - 3
9. I feel proud of my spending habits.		1 - 2 - 3
10. I know how much I am worth.		1 - 2 - 3
11. I am optimistic about my ability to increase my net worth.		1 - 2 - 3
12. I am clear about my financial goals and my plans to achieve them.		1 - 2 - 3
13. I contribute to causes that are important to me.		1 - 2 - 3
14. I feel prepared for retirement.		1 - 2 - 3
15. I feel assured that, if I died today, my affairs would be properly handled.		1 - 2 - 3
16. Overseeing my finances is a welcome challenge.		1 - 2 - 3

Add up the numbers you circled to determine your total score. TOTAL:

Scoring 18–30: You are in the danger zone. Unless you become better informed and are actively growing your money faster than inflation and taxes are taking it away, you are putting yourself in peril. Granted, you may not have a problem now, but the clock is ticking, the potential for disaster is there.

31–42: You're on the right track but not out of the woods. As Will Rogers once said, "Even if you are on the right track, you'll get run over if you just sit there." You've made some headway, but there's still more to do. Beware of the big trap at this point: It could be easy to ignore or minimize the need for further action, to convince yourself you don't need to worry yet. Remain vigilant in your efforts.

43–54: Consider yourself a smart woman. Short of a perfect score, however, there are still certain areas that require your attention. Even then, don't let your diligence slip by the wayside. Financial responsibility is a lifelong commitment. We can always continue to grow even smarter.

• • • • • • • • • • • • • • • •

The purpose of this quiz is to get a broad-brush view of your relationship with money as well as pinpoint any areas in which you feel less competent or weaker than others. A circled 1, even a 2, points to a trouble spot, where you are particularly vulnerable. Keep these statements in mind as you read this book.

Remember ...

1. Any woman can become financially adept.
2. You don't need a lot of money to begin.
3. Don't wait for a crisis to get started.

Part One

• •

THE PROBLEM

More women today have money than ever before. So what's the problem? For most of us, money promises fewer problems, greater freedom, and more security. In a *Ms.* magazine survey of 23,000 readers, a full 73 percent believed money would buy happiness. Yet for many women, having money in the bank is like finding a time bomb in the basement. They know they need to do something, but they haven't a clue what it is they need to do.

Chapter One

· ·

The Guide Makes the Journey

We look for money to give us what
we can only find inside.
—JACOB NEEDLEMAN

Growing up, I never thought much about money. I never needed to. Like water for a fish, it was always there. My father, Richard, is the R in H&R Block, the income tax preparation company he started with his brother, Henry. My father never seemed to have any difficulty with money—making it or managing it. But then again, he never really talked about money, except to complain when my mother spent too much. And my mother never talked about money either. She just loved to spend it. Even though I saw her at her desk in the living room, paying the bills every month, my father was the one who made all the major financial decisions. He was clearly in charge. And he did a great job. I felt absolutely secure knowing he was taking care of things. I always knew there would be plenty as long as he was in control.

I can still recall the first real conversation we had about money. It was my twenty-first birthday. My parents sent twenty-one bottles of wine (seven red, seven white, seven rosé) to my apartment at Boston University. Then their private jet picked me up at Logan Airport and flew me to Las Vegas, where they met me in a limousine. We stayed in a glorious suite atop Caesar's Palace, and on the morning of my birthday, we celebrated with lox, bagels, and champagne they had sent to the room.

Suddenly, in the middle of breakfast, Dad dropped a thick legal document on the table. No one said anything. I wasn't quite sure what was going on. Mom smiled knowingly. Finally Dad pointed to the papers and said, "You're a very rich girl, Barbara."

He explained that this was a trust document with several thousand shares of H&R Block stock. He probably explained a lot more, but I didn't hear any of it. I was stunned, overcome by a numb sense of unreality. I was rich! What did that mean? Slowly, the numbness turned into a kind of dreamlike euphoria.

"You'll never have to worry," I remember my dad saying that morning. It was the only advice my parents ever gave me about money. "Don't worry." Under those words, of course, was an unspoken assumption: "There will always be a man to take care of you." And they really believed it. After all, they were a product of their time. Mom had watched her mother make a weekly budget and then ask her husband for what she needed. Dad had seen his father take complete charge of the family's money, including his wife's inheritance. My parents both truly believed that my world would be safe because I had all this money and Dad would take care of everything until I married, at which time the responsibility, like a family coat of arms, would pass to my husband. That's how they had done it. That's how it was done. And I certainly showed no interest in learning about money. I didn't want anything to do with it. Money was too big a responsibility, and I felt utterly incapable.

My family genuinely believed, and so did I—though I never would have admitted it to anyone—that a woman's role was to take care of the house so the husband could succeed. Although I earned a master's degree in counseling psychology and ran my own career-consulting firm, my work, in everyone's eyes—including mine—always took a back seat to my husband's. How well I remember my mother's favorite mantra: "Behind every successful man there is a woman." Dad would smile that Cheshire cat grin of his whenever he heard her say it. We all knew what an important part Mom played in his success. She made sure everything ran smoothly. Dinner was on the table at exactly five forty-five every evening, when he got home; if there were ever any problems with us kids, she took care of them; when Dad needed her counsel, she was at his side to help him. She was a devoted mother, charming hostess, and wise advisor. But when it came to finances, Father knew best. That's the only model I had, not just in our house but on TV, in the movies, everywhere I looked: the man handled the money.

And it worked that way in my life . . . for a while. I remember the first time my family met the man I would eventually marry—a wonderfully handsome man I had met on a family trip to Israel. We were always taking family vacations, and my sisters and I were always having wild romances, but this one was different. I fell madly in love with a dashing dark-haired man with an exotic Israeli accent. Dad took him on a long walk during that first meeting.

When they returned, I quickly took my father aside. "What did you think of him?" I asked breathlessly.

"He's brilliant," my father exclaimed in approval.

And he *was* brilliant. Trained as a lawyer, he became a stockbroker and financial planner. Naturally, he took care of everything for me. I never paid a bill, balanced my checkbook, or saw the inside of a tax return. I'd just sign whatever he told me to sign. It was exactly as my parents had planned and exactly as I had expected.

However, money without responsibility is like a house of cards. One strong wind, one big crisis, and it all comes tumbling down. Even if nothing happens, even if all goes smoothly, as it did for me for many years, there is always that gnawing fear, unconscious though it may be, that whenever there is the slightest breeze, it may all blow away.

The First Clue

I remember, with chilling clarity, the first gust of wind, the first indication that maybe things weren't going so well. Late one evening, coming home from a long day at work, I walked in to find my parents sitting in the living room with my husband, everyone looking very serious, the tension almost unbearable.

"We need to talk, Barbara," Dad said in a stern voice. I glanced at my husband, who was staring intently at the floor. I lowered myself into a chair, my heart racing. What was going on? Dad's next words explained everything. "Did you know your husband has lost so much of your money in the stock market that you don't have enough left to buy a house?"

It was a left hook out of nowhere. Was this some kind of cruel joke? During all the months of house hunting, my husband had never mentioned watching costs, not even when we found a house we loved. Instead he went to my father for permission to take money from my trust. Thank goodness the trust was set up so no one could touch the principal until I turned forty.

My parents were furious, and justifiably so. This man was squandering the money they had worked hard for, this man they had trusted to take care of their daughter.

"Did you know he was doing this?" Dad demanded.

My reaction was instantaneous. "Yes," I lied, too embarrassed to admit that I didn't know what my husband was doing with my money. I felt humiliated, betrayed, and deeply ashamed. How could he have done this? How could I not have known?

After my parents left, my husband and I sat in stunned silence, as though there were a dead body on the floor and neither one of us knew what to do with it. Then the inevitable words pierced the quiet. "Don't worry," he said, almost pleading. He apologized, admitted he'd made a mistake, and swore he'd never play the stock market so foolishly again. I believed him. I had to. The thought of not being able to continue to count on him was inconceivable.

No one ever mentioned that incident again. I assumed my husband was true to his word. I didn't want to know otherwise. A few years went by. We moved from Kansas City to San Francisco. I wanted to live near the ocean and write. He wanted to buy a seat on the Pacific Stock Exchange and be in the center of the action on the trading floor.

It was during this period that something very curious happened. I had written a book, about job hunting, and wanted to write another, this one about career change. As a career counselor, I often gave lectures on this subject. I knew what I wanted to say. But when I tried to write, my mind went blank. The words came out stilted, forced, like trying to pull up weeds stubbornly rooted in the soil.

On the night of Rosh Hashanah—the beginning of the Jewish New

Year—my family and I had gone to temple, and now everyone was in bed, my husband beside me, my daughters each tucked away in their rooms, the house dark. I lay awake, talking to God, asking for help. Why was I so stuck? I wanted to know. Why couldn't I write this book? Tell me, I prayed, what did I need to do? Then—I didn't know why—I got out of bed and, like a puppet guided by invisible strings, walked into my study. Picking up a pen, I wrote: "To be a guide, you must first make the journey."

I read it several times. I wasn't used to receiving cosmic messages, but this was clearly a message: if not from the cosmos, then from my subconscious. The meaning was obvious, or so I thought. I wasn't yet ready to write. I hadn't finished my own transition. At the time, I thought it meant I hadn't completed my journey from career counselor to full-time writer. It made sense. So I set the book idea side and pretty much forgot about it, while I began taking writing classes, selling articles, and syndicating a business column in newspapers.

Meanwhile, my husband and I started arguing about money and how much I was spending. I felt that his accusations were completely unfounded. Yet the arguments rapidly escalated. I became suspicious. Was he losing money in the market again? I asked. He swore he wasn't, but his excuses weren't convincing. I suspected he was lying, but I didn't dare admit it. Wanting everything to be okay, I let it go. Over the years, we continued to have too many arguments about money; there were too many admonishments from him that we didn't have enough, too many explanations that didn't ring true. And yet I kept believing my husband's promises. I shudder now to think how insane that was. But then I was too scared to do anything. Like a child, I thought that if I closed my eyes the problem would go away. I can only guess, by my whole family's silence, that they felt the same way.

Awakening

Then one day my carefully constructed illusions abruptly disintegrated into dust. I went to the bank's ATM to take out some money—not more than $60—and a message on the screen told me I didn't have enough cash in my account to cover the withdrawal. I was startled. This was never supposed to happen. I put the plastic card in again, and then again. "Please," I prayed, "be a mistake." But the machine insisted it was right. I knew something was terribly wrong.

That moment at the ATM was about far more than a deficient bank balance. It was about denial. Or rather the end of denial—one of life's most painful experiences. Suddenly, with a minor incident like withdrawing cash from the bank, a truth I'd worked so long and hard to conceal was staring me in the face, like a hideous jack-in-the-box sprung out of hiding. I felt icy panic in my stomach. I knew I could no longer close my eyes.

"What's going on?" I demanded of my husband when he got home that evening.

"Don't worry," he said calmly. "I'll take care of it."

It was tempting to jump into those words as if they were a hot bath on a chilly morning. A part of me desperately wanted to stay submerged in my illusion of safety. As hard as it is to admit, there is something extremely seductive about ignorance. I clung to it like a security blanket, as if I could curl up in my illusion of safety, feeling sheltered and warm and taken care of, pretending everything would be okay and I didn't have to do a thing. Yet, as Buddha warned, at the root of all suffering is ignorance. My ignorance had indeed become a source of great suffering.

This time, however, the pain felt like scalding water. My pretenses began to melt, and the gripping fear wouldn't let me rest. I had to know the truth. Were we broke? At the time, I had no idea how much money I had or where it was. I felt like my husband talked in circles whenever I asked him about it. Unable to pin him down to specifics, I became frozen with terror. Then the panic gave way to numbness, as if I were sleepwalking through a horrible dream, hoping desperately it would end. But week after week, the ATM continued to insist I had insufficient funds. Too ashamed, too humiliated, to talk to my friends, I had no one to turn to. Who would understand?

About this time, my parents came to San Francisco for a visit. I was terrified to tell them, knowing how angry they would be. But the pressure inside me was intolerable. I had to talk to someone. We were standing in my kitchen, making breakfast. While buttering toast, I pulled the plug from the grenade.

"I-I think my husband is losing money again," I stammered. Sure enough, my father exploded.

"If you can't get your husband to be more responsible," he bellowed, "I am going to take the money away from you."

Years later, I found out he couldn't have done that. I had an irrevocable trust, which no one, not even my father, could change. But at that moment we were both reacting out of fear and helplessness. I could only scream back, "What about me? Why can't *I* manage the money?"

Dad looked dumbfounded. This thought was as strange, as unfathomable, to him as it was to me. Still, my managing money was the only solution either of us could think of. I asked him what I should do.

"Talk to people," he told me. "Ask questions."

"What questions?" I asked.

"Whatever you want to know," he answered impatiently.

I have looked back to that day from the distance of years and wondered why my father didn't help me more during that time, especially since it was his business to help others with their financial lives. But I think we were all suddenly catapulted into a situation so foreign that neither he nor Mom was prepared to deal with it. And on a deeper, subliminal level, I believe it was time to break my dependency on my parents, time for them to stop protecting me, time for me to learn a very fundamental lesson about self-reliance.

At that moment, however, I just wanted to be rescued. I didn't know what I needed to know. I hadn't the slightest idea whom to ask. I was scared. But worse, I felt stupid. I didn't realize then that there was a world of difference between being stupid and being uneducated.

The financial problems only exacerbated all the other problems in my marriage. Three months short of our fifteenth anniversary, I got a divorce. Now I was alone with three daughters, one just a baby, and I could no longer afford the luxury of not worrying.

Getting Help

What was I supposed to do now? In desperation, I made appointments with half a dozen financial advisors. I knew I needed a professional to help me. What I didn't expect was that the experience would be so intimidating. I felt very naive. They would ask me questions that I couldn't answer—simple questions like "How much money do you have?" Nor could I think of the right questions to ask them. So many of the experts I visited were pompous, insensitive, and condescending, even some of the women. After I briefly told one woman my story, I added, "I want to be educated. I need someone who will teach me about investing." In her ultra-chic Armani suit, her arms crossed, she scowled at me from behind her oversized, meticulously organized desk.

"You won't find any money manager who will take the time to teach you," she said, her voice patronizing. "If I want to buy you shares in IBM, I am not going to stop to ask you whether or not I should do it." I felt as if she had just slapped my hand and told me what a bad girl I was to even suggest such a thing.

But I kept at it, and finally I found Bob Lovett, an investment manager. He spent a great deal of time with me, without even knowing if he'd get my business. He gave me my first elementary course in understanding money. He told me what papers to bring him. He showed me how to interpret my trust statement. (Until Bob, I didn't even know I got statements from the bank that handled my trust.) And he told me what questions I should be asking. Half the time, I didn't understand what he said. Often I'd virtually block out his words. Other times it was as if he was speaking a foreign language. But I liked him and trusted him, so I gave him money to invest for me in the stock market.

Bob often sent me reports on how my stocks were doing. I'd throw them away unread. I just wanted to know that my investments were going up. He assured me they were. Life seemed to be getting better. At last I had found a man I could count on to take care of my money. But that was 1986. Less than a year later—October 19, 1987—the Dow-Jones crashed, plunging 500 points in one day. The media dubbed this day Black Monday. I panicked. I called Bob and told him to sell every stock I owned. He begged me not to, assuring me the stock market would eventually bounce back, that I would have a huge capital gains tax if I sold. I didn't know what capital gains meant, and I didn't care. Convinced the world was on the brink of disaster, I just wanted out, wanted my cash safe in some bank.

Only years later would I realize what a terrible mistake I had made.

Bob's predictions were right-on. The market indeed bounced back, even climbed higher, and the people who stayed in reaped the rewards. I ended up paying a lot of money to the government, because even with the crash, my portfolio made money that year. When I sold my stock, I had to pay taxes on the profits. But at the time, I didn't care about capital gains or anything else to do with money. I just wanted to close my eyes to the whole thing.

The Final Crisis

When life wants to teach us a lesson, I have come to believe, it won't let us keep our eyes closed for very long. Life has its ways of forcing us to pay attention, whether we want to or not. One day not long after the October crash, I got a letter from the state franchise tax board, written in ridiculously confusing language. I didn't understand a word it said, so I just tossed it onto a pile of tax-related papers and figured that eventually I'd show it to someone who would explain it to me. Tax time arrived, and I took all my papers to my accountant. He looked at the letter from the state, reread it carefully, then, with a very solemn expression, asked me if I had a good lawyer. "It looks like you owe the state $583,000," he said.

I quickly found a lawyer, who explained that in 1982, the year we moved west from Kansas, my husband didn't pay the State of California for the gains on a sale of H&R Block stock. Now, seven years later, with fines and penalties, I owed the state a bloody fortune. My ex-husband had moved back to Israel, so I was left to foot the bill.

My lawyers tried to fight it, but we lost. With money from my trust, I paid over half-million dollars to the government, plus a small fortune in legal fees. This was clearly my wake-up call. I needed to get smart about money—fast.

I signed up for a class in financial planning at a community college. I asked the trust officer at my bank for suggestions, and she told me to read Jane Bryant Quinn's book on money. I talked to all kinds of financial advisors. But whatever they explained, whatever I read, I forgot the next day. I even took the H&R Block tax course, and I failed every single test. (One of the few questions I answered correctly had to do with owing taxes to the State of California.) I figured my brain wasn't equipped to absorb this kind of information. Maybe it was a genetic deficiency. Slowly, I slipped back into denial.

The years passed. Life went on. Until one fateful January day in 1990, when I received another letter, this one from the Internal Revenue Service. Again, I couldn't understand it, but at least I was smart enough now not to toss it aside. I immediately took it to a financial planner, one of the legion of people I had consulted to learn about finances.

"Uh-oh," he gulped. This time I owed $643,000 for a tax shelter my husband had gotten us into in 1979, which had been declared illegal. I had never heard of this tax shelter, but my signature was on the partnership agreement. No surprise. I had signed without question everything my husband handed me. Now, with my ex-husband unreachable in Israel, I was the one who had to pay back the original investment, plus the killer fines and penalties.

This time, the outcome was critical. Paying the full amount would put me in a really serious financial bind. I was scared. I hadn't talked to my parents about money—or anything else, for that matter—since my divorce. Filled with anger and bitterness, I blamed them for not preparing me to handle money. My wrath had pushed them away. But now I was terrified. If I had to pay this bill, my trust would be significantly depleted. There was no way I could support my children on the money I made as a writer. I called my father. I knew that despite our estrangement, he would rescue me. I knew he would lend me money. But I was wrong. He flat out refused.

I was stunned, consumed with fury and fear. "What will I do if I have to pay?" I wailed over the phone.

"Live on less," he answered curtly.

"I'm not supposed to worry about this stuff, remember?" I screamed as I slammed down the phone.

All of a sudden everything changed. My faith had been ruptured. My cocoon began unraveling. I made one last frantic attempt to get help. I phoned my ex-husband in Israel. I begged him to write a letter to the IRS, explaining that I had had no idea what I was signing.

"Then I'll have to pay," he snapped. "I don't have that kind of money."

"Please," I implored him. "Just think about it."

Well, he thought about it. Then, being a former lawyer, he drafted a legal brief, which he sent to the IRS. In it, he methodically explained how I knew exactly what I was signing, that my father founded H&R Block, and that I had an extensive knowledge of such financial matters.

At the time, I was wild with anger at my ex-husband's behavior, furious at myself for being so naive, and seething at a system that seemed so unfair. Eventually, however, my rage subsided, washed away by torrents of sorrow, desperation, and loneliness. Only now do I recognize that the refusal to help by these men in my life was a gift in disguise. It was the turning point for me, the moment when I knew that no one—not my former husband, not my lawyers, not even my father—would save me. It was up to me to do something. That realization, devastating as it was, actually set me free. Until I came to it, I remained chained to the past, unmotivated to change, unable to move forward.

It reminds me of a story. A young man once approached Buddha and asked what he must do to obtain enlightenment. Buddha took the man to the river and told him to submerge himself. When the young man did as he was told, Buddha held his head under the water until he was frantically gasping for air. "Why did you do that?" the young man sputtered breathlessly when Buddha finally released him. "When you want enlightenment as much as you wanted air," was the answer, "then you will find it."

I wanted financial enlightenment that badly. In my mind, I was fighting for survival. If I didn't do something, I would go under, and I would take my three daughters with me. My biggest fear, a haunting fear, was that any day I would go back to the ATM and once again be told I had no money. I vowed to change. And gradually, things did start changing. My lawyer gathered enough evidence to miraculously negotiate with the IRS. The final bill was a fraction of what they originally demanded. Grateful that I wasn't destitute, I was now determined to learn. Getting smart had taken on a new sense of urgency.

Taking Charge

I knew my reprieve was only temporary. If I didn't start taking control of my money, I'd lose it, all of it. There would be another tax bill, a market crash, or some other crisis. Deep in my bones, I felt that a disaster could be averted if I took action. I knew it was up to me. Every single loss I had incurred was the result of my failure to take responsibility for my finances.

This realization didn't come quickly. I spent years blaming my ex-husband, furious with him for the harm he had done. I was enraged at my parents because they hadn't taught me about money or protected me when they knew what was happening. I swung from fits of rage to torrents of self-pity, feeling like a helpless, hopeless victim. But eventually it hit me. *They* didn't do anything to me. *I* did it to me, through my ignorance, my denial, my failure to take charge. Now I had three daughters depending on me. Did I want to jeopardize their security? What kind of role model was I? Was I the kind of woman I wanted them to be?

During this difficult period, I kept a quote by Harriet Beecher Stowe tacked on the wall by my desk: "When you get into a tight place and everything goes against you, till it seems as though you could not hold on a minute longer, never give up, for that is the time and place the tide will turn."

Sure enough, it was right there, when I was at my lowest ebb, that the tide began to turn, in a way I could never have predicted. I was having lunch with a friend, Tracy Gary, founder of Resourceful Women, a nonprofit organization dedicated to the financial education of women. She told me they were looking for a writer to research and write about the issues and challenges that wealthy women encounter. "Why don't you apply?" she suggested. Why not? I called the next day for an interview, and within a week I was hired. For the next several months, I interviewed thirty women—fifteen who inherited money and fifteen who earned it. All of them were smart with money.

The research was fascinating. But its effect on me was totally unexpected. In the interviews, each woman would tell me her story, how she got smart with money. "So that's how you do it," I would say to myself. I felt as if I had stumbled on one of man's greatest and mostly closely held secrets.

All the books I read, all the classes I attended, had told me that learning about money was a matter of education. "Just start," the experts proclaimed. But the people who wrote the books and gave the lectures were experts. The material was easy and familiar, was second nature to them. It would be like a master chef handing a complicated gourmet recipe to a novice and saying, "Just start." To the novice, it's overwhelming. To the chef, it's simply part of a day's work.

In these women's stories, however, I got to see what "just start" actually meant, what it looked like to go from being financially stupid to being financially savvy. Each of these women had been ignorant about money in the beginning. Yet each one had become knowledgeable and competent. I was galvanized by the confidence and power that getting smart had given them. I coveted their ability, their confidence, their impact. I knew I was learning the mysteries of money from them.

Reaching Out

I started to search for patterns. What did these women have in common? Was it the way they were raised? Was it something in their character? Were there certain actions they all took or certain ways of thinking they shared?

It took me a while to find the answers to these questions. But something incredible happened almost immediately. Suddenly what was once inconceivable—that I could be smart with money—became a possibility. These women, in sharing their stories, encouraged me, inspired me, gave me hope and a way to start. After hearing their mistakes, their first fumbling steps, their awkwardness, their discomfort, along with their determination to keep plowing forward, I felt truly encouraged. I decided to tackle the subject again. This time, however, whenever I wanted to throw up my hands in frustration or confusion, I remembered so many of those women describing the same feelings, and I wouldn't give up. Gradually, what was once gibberish started making sense. For the first time, I was excited about the subject.

These interviews were like healthy amphetamines, and I was hooked. I felt energized, eager, wanting more. I started talking to my women friends about money, sharing my fears and struggles as well as my revelations. A few would get a glazed look in their eyes, nod politely, and change the subject. But most were eager to discuss this verboten topic with someone. Men sit around and gab about the stock market or their latest financial deals. But managing money is not something women talk about very much. While men are trading hot tips, we're gossiping about hot dates. How often, over a cup of coffee or a glass of wine, do we lean toward a girlfriend and say, "I just discovered a mutual fund that's beating the indexes by 5 percent." Or, "I'm thinking about putting some money in Exxon. What do you think?" Or even, "I want to get into the market. How did you start?" Which is exactly what I began doing during lunch dates or phone conversations.

My friends were not particularly rich. Most were earning a living, many were making good money, and while some were very knowledgeable, a lot of them wanted to ignore their financial life, just as I had all those years. Yet, like myself, many were feeling the consequences of their avoidance. One of my closest friends was on the verge of bankruptcy. "I feel like I've been brainwashed," she confided to me, close to tears. "I am phenomenally uninformed about money, but I don't know where to start." Another friend, single and almost sixty, knew she should begin planning for retirement, but she was overwhelmed by all the choices. "I don't know what to do, so I don't do anything at all," she lamented. Both were successful in their careers but had been totally indifferent to what it meant to take financial responsibility.

I met many more women like them. I saw the pain and difficulties they suffered because they never got a grip on their finances. If only they could have the kind of role models I had encountered in my research, I remember thinking. Then I got a phone call that gave me an idea. Anne, who had typed the transcripts of my Resourceful Woman interviews, called me.

"I've just got to tell you," she said exuberantly. "I was so inspired by reading those interviews that I went out and found a stockbroker. I don't have a lot of money, but I have more than I ever had before, and now I realize I need to do something."

As she read those women's stories, Anne told me, she saw beyond her preconceived ideas about money for the first time. She understood that though she was married, she needed to be fiscally responsible. She recognized she had choices that she hadn't been aware of before. And she knew what to do. While I listened to her, the idea for this book started taking shape.

Remembering the message I had received years before, late that Rosh Hashanah night, I saw how far I'd come. I felt I had "made the journey," though it was clearly an ongoing one. I was finally getting my financial act together. I sensed that the time had come to write a book based on what I'd learned about money.

Yet when I sat down at the computer, I found myself stuck again. Here it was a decade—it seemed a lifetime—later, and I was experiencing déjà vu. Again I talked to God, and again I pleaded for help. But this time there was no cosmic message, only a chance meeting with an old friend. Judy Barber, a family therapist who specializes in money issues, was lecturing at a financial retreat I was attending. I had known Judy for years, but we rarely saw each other. We agreed to meet the next day for an early-morning hike. Walking briskly over the grassy hills in the Sonoma wine country that cool spring morning, I told Judy that I had been trying to write a book about women and money but was stuck.

"Maybe you could help me figure out what's stopping me," I suggested. The words slipped out unexpectedly, surprising even me.

She hesitated, then laughed. "I know I can help people with their blocks around money," she said, "but I've never helped anyone with their blocks around a book on money." She agreed to try, however, and I made an appointment to come to her office the next week. The session lasted an hour and a half. Prodded by her gentle but insightful questions, I made an unexpected discovery.

"I'm afraid," I admitted haltingly, "that if I tell my story, I will hurt my parents." With those words came the tears. After all the years spent in anger and blame against my family for not preparing me to manage money, I had finally come to see that their intentions were loving and their actions well-meaning. They had been as victimized by cultural attitudes as I had. We had all grown and matured from our experiences. Today my parents are as supportive and understanding as I could ever want them to be.

I learned, ultimately, a lot of valuable lessons from my parents, many of which I share in this book. For one, I understand the benefits of investing for one's future security. I have learned the value of frugality and good spending habits, without which wealth would be impossible. And I have discovered, through their example, the importance of philanthropy to causes that have deep personal meaning, of giving back to a world that has given us so much.

Above all, I have come to see that when a woman paves her own way, she doesn't have to lose the ones she loves. But she must get to the point where she is willing to let go of everything in order to find the strength and independence within herself. Only then, fortified by her own convictions, will she see her relationships powerfully transformed into richer, deeper, more profoundly loving ones than she had ever before thought possible.

It is with this awareness that I share my story in this book, as others have shared theirs with me. My dream is that, inspired by the candor and intimacy of these personal stories, we will begin to seek out other women, frankly discuss our financial affairs, combine our resources, knowledge, and creativity, and give one another emotional as well as practical support. It is by talking openly among ourselves that we as women will truly make our impact on the world.

Chapter Two

• •

If I'm So Smart, Why Am I So Dumb About Money?

Ask not the sparrow how the eagle soars, for those with little wings have not accepted for themselves the power to share with you.
—A COURSE IN MIRACLES

Once, years ago, I had a chance encounter that epitomizes for me the modern woman's financial struggle. I was speaking to a local women's group about my research for the Resourceful Women project. An acquaintance I hadn't seen for years was in the audience. Gayle, a lovely, unassuming woman, was a writer who had the enviable distinction of actually having made a lot of money from her writing. Besides authoring six books, she had designed several software programs, and she published a monthly newsletter. Clearly this woman was no slouch. She listened with rapt attention during my talk, and afterward she rushed over, eager to speak to me. "I am going right from here to Charles Schwab," she declared excitedly. "I've put off doing this long enough!"

"That's great," I exclaimed, thrilled the discussion had inspired her to visit a brokerage firm. This was exactly the kind of impact I hoped for in addressing these groups. "Let me know how it goes," I called to her as she hurried out the door. I didn't hear from her until she phoned me a month later. This time, however, there was none of her earlier enthusiasm.

She had gone to Charles Schwab, she told me, but had walked out in a daze. The account application she had taken with her remained blank. That same day, she had also subscribed to the *Wall Street Journal*, but she had yet to read one issue.

"Dealing with money makes me want to cry," she blurted out. "I'm so afraid I'll do something dumb and it will all go down the drain. What frightens me more than anything is the thought of being destitute. Nothing else scares me so much—not death, disease, or pain. Only poverty and old age. I don't know what to do, so I do nothing at all." Just past sixty, Gayle had no funds set aside for retirement.

I knew this was more than one woman's cry for help. In Gayle, I saw myself and countless others: intelligent women who feel financially stupid. When it comes to money, we zone out, fog up, or shut down. The more women I talked to, the more I observed this same reaction. Their stories were variations on a single theme—they were unprepared, ill equipped, and downright afraid to handle their finances. It didn't matter whether they were young or old, married or single, supported by a spouse, earning their own livelihood, or living off a trust fund. They were struggling with what has become an increasingly pressing problem for a woman in today's world.

A Look on the Bright Side

Once upon a time, the man made the money and the woman married the man. That road to riches, however, is rapidly changing. Today more women have money than ever before. I'm not talking about access to someone else's money. We have our own sources of discretionary income, not to mention retirement funds. As the *Wall Street Journal* has pointed out, until recently "widows and wealthy divorced women . . . tended to be the only women with substantial amounts of money. . . . But these days, lots of women have money."

Never in our history have women had more opportunities to strike it rich on our own. In fact, women have a higher net worth than men. Forty-two percent of Americans with gross assets of $600,000 or more are women. Clearly we've taken immense strides away from the not so distant past, when women weren't allowed to own property, work outside the home, even have a bank account or credit card in their own name. (As recently as 1930, twenty-six states prohibited married women from working.)

Today 55 percent of employed women bring in half or more of their household income, and one out of four working wives outearn their husbands. Sure, women as a whole still earn less than men. But we are quickly catching up. As we become better educated and more experienced in the workplace, our earnings rise accordingly. Already, the number of women doctors has doubled, women lawyers have quadrupled, and female officers from the position of vice president and up in Fortune 500 companies have almost tripled. The top women in corporate America have seen their salaries double in the past ten years, to average $187,000 annually. (This figure lags behind what male executives are raking in, and men clearly outnumber women in those senior positions, but still, on any chart, the increase is noteworthy.)

Of even greater significance than our presence in the corporate world is the proliferation of women-owned businesses. Women are making virtual fortunes as entrepreneurs. Profits from these ventures, which are growing four times faster than businesses owned by men, are, according to the National Foundation for Women Business Owners, generating $1.4 trillion in annual revenue. By the year 2000, over 50 percent of all firms will be female owned.

Add to that another statistic in the "good news" column. This has to do with women who are inheriting their fortunes. In this decade alone, an astounding $8 trillion will transfer to a younger generation, with 55 percent going to women.

Now for the Bad News

But there is a somber side to this rosy picture. *Despite our economic gains, we are not protecting ourselves financially.* I vividly remember interviewing June, a middle-aged woman who inherited a sizable fortune.

"When my parents died," June told me, "I was selling hosiery in a department store. Between my husband and me, we earned $40,000. Suddenly I had a two-million-dollar inheritance. I panicked. I felt like the dumbest person in the world. None of my friends had money, so I didn't tell anyone. I was sure they'd say, 'I wish I had your problems.' I didn't know who I could trust. I had no one to talk to. I didn't know what to do with all that money. I was terrified I'd make a mistake and blow it."

A lot of people would find it hard to fathom that someone inheriting millions could be worried about money. Yet affluence doesn't eliminate anxiety. As an article in *USA Today* revealed, even the rich worry about money. "A survey of the wealthiest one percent of Americans—those with at least $200,000 a year income or $3 million net worth—found that most fear they won't have enough for retirement." Indeed, June and others are right to be concerned. Too many well-heeled but uninformed women allow themselves to be lulled into a false sense of safety because they inherit a bundle, earn a nice income, anticipate a fat pension, or marry a rich man. But their financial ignorance jeopardizes their future security. Sadly, thousands of women do "blow it." Not even the wealthy are immune.

"Every morning, I wake up feeling like there's ground glass in my gut," Audrey confessed to me. "I'm making good money, but I have nothing to show for it. I work twenty hours a day, seven days a week. I thought that the more I worked, the more I earned, the more I would have. But that isn't the case. I'm totally broke, and nobody knows it."

This woman's plight reveals a tragic fact. *Just because we have money doesn't mean we'll keep it.* There is a big difference between having money and holding on to it. Hoping to preserve our money without any financial skills is like trying to hold water in a sieve. We'll wind up watching our dollars go down the drain, washed away by neglect, overspending, or following bad advice. We stand to lose not only our money but our peace of mind as well.

The important truth is that large bank balances are no guarantee of financial security or financial savvy. "I have clients who have seven-digit incomes, and they don't feel capable of managing their money," says Kathleen Gurney, a financial psychologist. Even women who oversee large budgets at work feel helpless when it comes to their own financial affairs.

"I manage $10 million in my job, and I don't even know what a mutual fund is," one such businesswoman declared. "It makes me realize how vulnerable I am."

Women today are vulnerable. Like Gayle, many of us, when we don't know what to do, do nothing at all—until hit with an emergency or impending retirement. Then it may be too late. In the eye of a crisis or on the brink of old age is the worst time to play catch-up.

Until we take seriously the need to get smart about money—regardless of how much we have or how we come by it—we may find ourselves teetering precariously over a very unknown future. Without a safety net to catch them, already many women are falling on hard times. And a lot of us are scared. A *Working Woman* magazine survey reveals that one out of every two of its readers—women with incomes four times higher than the average—worries about becoming a bag lady. Unfortunately, it's a valid concern.

I'll never forget a conversation with a former housewife who had lived in a big house in an exclusive suburb until her husband left her. "Suddenly I had to go on food stamps to support my three children," she told me, close to tears. "It was so scary to have no money and no one to bail me out. All I could think was: If I'm so smart, why am I so dumb about money?"

A lot of women ask themselves that same question. And indeed, we must wonder why this is so. Why do so many smart, successful women lack the competence and confidence to deal with their finances? Why do so many once-prosperous women end up impoverished? The solution to the problem, I believe, lies in the answer to these questions. If we can figure out why we feel dumb about money, we will discover how to finally get smart with it. As I see it, the answer is twofold, both practical and psychological.

The Practical Aspect: No One Taught Us

This is the most obvious explanation for our financial ignorance: We've never been taught. We don't understand what it means to be smart with money. We have no road maps, so to speak. We have no role models.

Actually, society has taught us about money by not teaching us—what psychologists call "learned helplessness." We've been conditioned not to take responsibility. We may have seen our mothers pay the bills and balance the checkbooks, but our fathers were the breadwinners and decision makers. It wasn't long ago, 1984, that Clarence Pendleton of the U.S. Civil Rights Commission declared equal pay for equal work to be "the looniest idea since Looney Tunes came on the screen."

But times have changed. Most people don't consider women making and managing money such a loony idea anymore. In an Oppenheimer Management Corporation survey of two thousand people, 90 percent of the women and 85 percent of the men said managing money is *not* just a man's job. In a survey of over four thousand women sponsored by Prudential Securities, 94 percent believed they were as up to the task as men. The majority of women say *they want to take charge. They just don't know how.*

More and more, financial professionals are realizing this. Women are a hot commodity in the financial services industry. Indeed, a whole industry has sprung up to help damsels in financial distress. Look at all the services, publications, and courses marketed to women only. An article in the *Wall Street Journal* reported that women's groups have received an explosion of requests to provide financial seminars. Financial professionals wait like vultures to swoop down on any woman who says she needs help. The danger is that women will become easy prey for unscrupulous professionals. There's another danger. Women read these publications, attend the seminars (supposedly designed exclusively for women, yet offering the same information they give men), and still can't seem to make any headway. A woman's first reaction is often: "Something is wrong with me. I'm just not smart enough." Our ignorance feels inescapable, so we throw in the towel. "What's the use?" we say, turning our backs on our bank accounts.

Nothing is wrong with us. We're not stupid. We're just uninformed. We're operating within a narrow definition based on outdated memories and outmoded beliefs about what it means to take the financial reins.

What Does It Mean to Be Smart About Money?

McCall's magazine recently did a survey revealing that the majority of women think that if they understand a little bit about money management—like how to balance a checkbook, deposit a paycheck, or calculate their net worth—they feel they know enough. "Women tend to assume they know more than they do about financial management, often mistaking household money management with long-term asset building," the survey concluded.

In a separate study, *Money* magazine noted that women regard good money management in short-range terms, while men take a long-range view. In other words, according to a Merrill Lynch brokerage firm study, women set aside less of already lower incomes and are more apt to save for their children, a home, or a car than for retirement. Evidently, most women think they're doing fine if they can save money, make a major purchase, hunt for bargains, or earn a decent wage.

A decade or so ago, perhaps this *was* all a woman needed to know to get by. Nowadays, however, a smart woman must think beyond being a wage earner and a dollar watcher. She must also see herself as a wealth builder. Wealth builder? At the mere mention of the word "wealth," many of us immediately recoil. "Wealthy" conjures up images of Hollywood stars, Wall Street tycoons, or society matrons, and we instantly exclude ourselves from the possibility.

Or we look around and see all the hungry and homeless, all the excess and greed. Seeking wealth seems selfish, immoral, shameless. As one woman wrote in a letter to *Ms.* magazine: "Every day I see homeless people in need which makes me aware of how much I have, but not happier. I couldn't stand to be rich while others are poor."

Her view is a common one: "If I have less, someone will have more." It is, however, a misconception. Depriving ourselves will never enrich another.

"Wealth doesn't create poverty. It creates prosperity," proclaimed a *Forbes* magazine article. The article noted that during the 1980s, a decade notorious for "obscene wealth," there were more jobs, housing, and charitable giving than ever before. Of course, prosperity can easily disintegrate into avarice and extravagance. At the same time, prosperity paves the way for philanthropy.

Indeed, the whole concept of wealth, and what it means to create wealth, is a commonly misunderstood notion. Ask ten people what "wealthy" means, and you'll get ten different answers. A philosophic friend once told me, "Wealth is when you have a dollar more than you need"; whereas an heiress I knew to be worth millions said bluntly, "If I had a billion dollars, then I'd be wealthy." A businesswoman I interviewed said she would feel wealthy "when I make my first million." Yet another seemed to think one million dollars was nice, but not enough to qualify her as wealthy. And another happily told me she finally felt wealthy because she could walk into a store, buy what she wanted, and not have to rush home and figure out how to fit it into her budget.

Creating wealth doesn't mean you have to make millions (or marry a millionaire). Wealth has nothing to do with the size of your paycheck, an inheritance, or lottery winnings. One can earn a lot of money and still not be wealthy. Conversely, one can have a modest salary and create wealth.

Wealth is not so much what you have. Wealth comes from what you *do* with what you have. You create wealth by investing, or putting your money into assets that will grow. This is what the *McCall's* survey referred to, and what smart people understand as "long-term asset building." Oseola McCarty, an eighty-eight-year-old cleaning lady, made the news when she set up a $150,000 scholarship fund for minority students. Where did she get all that money, earning only $10 an hour washing people's clothes? By following the advice of bank officials who told her to invest conservatively. "It's not the ones who make big money but the ones who know how to save that get ahead," Oseola wisely explained.

Women have come to a relatively new juncture in their economic development. We now know how to work for our money. Next we need to understand how to make our money work for us. Getting smart with money means discovering the power of passive income.

Terry Savage, financial talk show host and well-known author, put it well during our interview when she reflected on her own career. Savage began as a secretary in a brokerage firm and became the first woman trader at the Chicago Options Exchange.

"The first generation of us started out just getting jobs," she reflected. "It was a big deal for me to be accepted as a trader. The next generation of us fought to get the right pay for the jobs. Not just the title, but the real commensurate pay that went with the responsibilities we had. Now the challenge for women is to do what men learned long ago: to make the money work as hard for us as we work for it. That's the real challenge."

Why Is Investing So Important?

Most of us know the value of savings. Experts generally recommend setting aside three to six months of living expenses for emergencies. But after that, then what? Should we be putting all our discretionary cash— what's left over at the end of the month after we've paid the bills, including all our unmortgaged debts—into a savings account? The answer is an unequivocal *no*.

Leaving that money in the bank is like putting a wool sweater in a hot dryer. If we let it sit too long, it will shrink before our very eyes. Why? Simply put: taxes and inflation. Every year, a big chunk of our money is eaten up by these two culprits. Right now, as I write, inflation hovers around 3 percent. If inflation remains at this modest rate, a dollar today will be worth only fifty cents in twenty years. But if inflation swells to 5 percent, which is more likely, that same dollar will shrivel to thirty-seven cents' worth in twenty years. In other words, two decades from now, a $40 pair of jeans will cost anywhere from $80 to $110. And even with a consistently low 3 percent inflation, a $30,000 car will cost $79,000 in twenty years, $129,658 in thirty years, and $201,143 in forty years. How many of us can count on salary increases at that level? Especially when studies show that women's earning power declines significantly as we age. Yet our life spans are increasing. *One of the greatest dangers we face is that we will outlive our money.*

Even if we can barely make ends meet as it is, even if we don't have any discretionary income, we are not off the hook. We still must become knowledgeable about investing. Chances are, if we work, we have an IRA, a 401(k), or some other tax-deferred retirement plan. More and more, the burden for managing these plans is falling on us, the employees. And the whopping majority of us are doing a lousy job preparing for old age. As was mentioned in the Introduction, studies consistently show that the bulk of retirement programs are either underfunded or poorly managed. Sadly, seven out of ten women never retire—because they can't afford to. This is a depressing statistic. To protect our future and ensure our peace of mind, we must take an active role in creating wealth. Interestingly, the root word for wealth is "weal," meaning well-being.

These warnings are nothing new. Most of us have heard them all many times but have yet to pay them heed. Why is this? The answer to that question, I believe, contains the crux of the problem confronting most women.

The Psychological Aspect: Why More Women Aren't Smart About Money

"There is nothing about money that cannot be understood by a person of reasonable curiosity, diligence, and intelligence," Harvard economist John Kenneth Galbraith once said. Or, as stockbroker Esther Berger succinctly summed it up: "This is not rocket science."

While it may be true that investing is not rocket science, it sure feels like it to a lot of us. Survey after survey reveals that women are intimidated by the investment world. *Self* magazine studied 1,376 women aged eighteen to forty-nine, of whom a full 36 percent said they were confident about buying insurance or committing to a mortgage, but only 19 percent were confident about buying stocks. And when the Oppenheimer Management Corporation asked two thousand people about their investment strategies, 71 percent of the women between the ages of thirty-five and fifty-four didn't know how to invest at all.

"Women, despite ever evolving attitudes, education, and training, still generally have major problems when dealing with the purchase of intangibles, such as stocks, bonds, or mutual funds," according to a *Los Angeles Times* news story.

What really astounds me is the number of female financial professionals I've met who have as much trouble as the rest of us. Just recently, an accountant told me, "Money is something I hold at arms' length. I am much better with other people's money than mine." A friend who was formerly employed on Wall Street admitted, "I was trading $500 million a day, and I can't even balance my checkbook." Another, the director of an MBA program who teaches finance and accounting, confessed, "My personal finances are a mess." And this from a venture capitalist: "I am really good in the business world. I can raise all kinds of money for people, deal in complicated transactions. But it's like my head doesn't follow through. It just isn't integrated with the rest of me."

These women should know better, right? In a rational world, yes. But rarely is taking financial responsibility a purely rational exercise. These women shed light on a fact that financial education programs, even those aimed specifically at women, tend to ignore. *It takes more than mechanics to learn about money.* Factual information does little to change years of conditioning. There is a colossal psychological component that casts a dark shadow over our financial dealings. For many of us, getting smart with money is as much about conquering fear and overcoming resistance as about learning facts and managing assets.

How do we know when it's an emotional issue we're dealing with rather than merely a matter of financial know-how? If we find ourselves fogging up or spacing out, if we can't seem to apply the information we learn, or resist learning it in the first place, then we've got our first clues. Chances are, psychological factors are impeding our progress.

Often when a woman attempts to take financial control, she is struck by a strong, even if fleeting, sense of foreboding—as if she is entering a place she shouldn't be, and somewhere deep in her psyche, an alarm goes off, warning, Danger! Keep out! As an instinctive act of self-protection, she shuts down, fogs up, or spaces out.

I watched this phenomenon strikingly reenacted during a conversation I had with a good friend. She had made a substantial sum of money in the past several years, which a financial advisor was managing for her. One day over lunch, I asked how her investments were doing. "Gosh, I don't know," she stammered, as she lowered her eyes and began fiddling with her hair. Suddenly I was witnessing a poised, supremely confident, sophisticated businesswoman turning into an awkward little girl.

I knew exactly what she was doing—I had done it myself so many times. I couldn't help but say something. "You're doing just what my friend David told me I did," I exclaimed. "He said, 'When you talk about money, Barbara, you go stupid. I know you're not stupid, but right now you're going stupid.'"

My friend looked at me, dumbfounded. "You're right," she admitted. "I do it a lot." Just recently, she told me, her twenty-five-year-old son, who worked for a brokerage firm, had tried to explain some financial concept to her. "I want you to get this," he had insisted. She listened intently, but when he finished, as she told me, "I hadn't heard a word he said. I went into this haze. I felt so stupid." She shook her head absently. "Why do I do this?" she wondered aloud.

At that moment, the loud wail of a siren interrupted our conversation. We glanced out the window, spied an ambulance racing by, and, when the wail subsided, went on talking, but about something totally unrelated to money. We hadn't spoken more than a few sentences, when I suddenly recognized the metaphor in what had just happened.

I interrupted my friend midsentence. "This is exactly what we do. Whenever we start to look at our money, I mean really look at money, it's like an alarm goes off and we shut down." I leaned across the table. "You know that conversation you had with your son?" She nodded. "Suppose your gynecologist was trying to explain something about your body, and he said, 'I want you to get this.' I bet you'd understand. And if you didn't, you'd keep asking questions until you did."

The Ultimate Taboo

Why do so many of us draw a blank when we talk about money? Why do we feel a foreboding, or some inexplicable sense of danger, when we step into the financial realm? Why does a woman who handles large budgets at work or is a financial professional feel like a "klutz," as one such woman put it, when it comes to *her own* money?

Perhaps there *is* a danger in learning about our finances. Think about it for a moment. What may happen if we get smart about money? For starters, we are likely to become financially responsible and economically independent. In our world, however, a financially self-sufficient woman is considered by many to be the ultimate taboo.

To understand why this is so, look at how our society has been structured for eons. Since humanity's beginnings, men and women have lived together in symbiotic relationships. We depend on men for physical and financial protection, while men depend on us for nesting and emotional nurturing. There was a time when this system made sense, when our survival depended on such a division of labor. Obviously the world has changed, but our mind-set hasn't.

What happens if one member of a symbiotic duo decides to change the contract? If a woman becomes financially independent, if she can take care of herself and her children on her own, then she no longer needs a man as she previously did, in the traditional sense, to take care of her. This prospect can be very threatening to men. Ironically, it is equally threatening to women.

"If I'm too successful," my friend Suzanne admitted to me, "no one will be there to take care of me." I heard similar comments from a multitude of women. A brokerage firm executive told me, "I was afraid that if I made too much money, a man would find me threatening. And I wanted a partner so badly that I held myself back in terms of income." And a struggling businesswoman summed up the dilemma this way: "I'm in a real Catch-22. You can either have a man or have money. Not both."

These women, and thousands like them, are facing a choice they should never have to make. "Whether they realize it or not," writes Annette Lieberman in *Unbalanced Accounts*, "these women are still collaborating with the myth that is the basis for the economic lives of middle-class women—that if they remain ladylike and needy, someone will take care of them. Because they associate financial rescue, or living happily ever after, with satisfaction of other emotional needs. They are afraid that abandoning the rescue fantasy also means abandoning the possibility of love."

"Our unarticulated fear," explains psychologist Sonya Freeman, "is that if we become more independent, others will view us as being able to take care of ourselves, in which case they will be free to leave us."

This fear of abandonment—which has been transmitted to us by our culture, our families, even our peers—is so embedded in our psyches that women themselves will sabotage success rather than break the taboo, which defines our boundaries like a barbed-wire fence. Whenever we try to cross into new financial territory, we are immediately warned, Keep out!

Few of us are consciously aware that the taboo operates so profoundly in our lives. But if we look closely, we'll see signs that it's there. We can spot it couched in phrases like: "I don't have time to deal with my finances," or "I don't have enough money to be bothered," or "That's just not the way I was raised."

I once heard a woman say, "It's okay to want jewelry or paintings or designer dresses. But just plain money making money—that seems so wrong. I know it makes no sense. But emotionally that's the way I am."

Many smart women I talked to were battling the taboo without even realizing it. But if I asked about it point-blank, which I almost always did, the fact invariably slipped out.

I remember one interview with a very sophisticated investor. Naomi was a sharp and determined woman, with a huge mane of hair and a surplus of confidence. Not quite forty years old, she had worked hard to become financially savvy, earning an MBA and starting her own trucking firm. Her efforts had paid off handsomely. She ran an extremely lucrative business in a male-dominated industry and successfully handled all the finances for her husband and her three children.

"I manage all the money in our house," she told me. "I make the investments. I decide our insurance needs. I handle our bank accounts. I guess I'm just not afraid of it." She paused briefly, then added proudly, "And I do a very good job."

"Do you ever feel, as a woman, that you shouldn't be handling money?" I asked her.

"Never," she responded adamantly. "I was raised to be responsible."

Later, as our conversation was winding up and I was gathering together my notes and tape recorder, I offhandedly asked how she felt about our interview.

"Embarrassed," she said, and then giggled.

"Embarrassed?" I repeated. I was genuinely surprised by the change in her demeanor. "Why?"

She thought about it for a while. "It's embarrassing for me to acknowledge the effort I've put into finances. If you have it all together and you let people know, you're being a braggart. You're supposed to be modest, to not let on."

"Could it be you're not supposed to be powerful?" I suggested. "Do you think there's something in our culture, a taboo, not so much against us handling money, but against us having power?"

"That's it!" she exclaimed. "I live with this feeling that it's somehow wrong to have spent so much time on this, that there is this value judgment from the outside world. I feel there is something wrong with me, that I'm different."

I asked her if she ever wanted to hold back.

"Oh, yes," she said, and she laughed somewhat sheepishly. "I want everybody to like me, be happy with me. There's a part of me that wants that above all."

Naomi is no different from anyone. All of us, men and women alike, want love and approval. Perhaps that's what keeps many of us trapped within the confines of what's acceptable. Perhaps that's why a *Working Woman* survey found that many readers had secret bank accounts their husbands knew nothing about. These were sophisticated women in managerial and entrepreneurial positions. Though smart enough to know they needed money in their own names, they weren't able to be up front about it with their husbands. Why? Perhaps they were afraid financial independence would endanger their relationships.

In a way, it's true. Breaking the taboo means shattering the very foundation on which our personal identity, our relationships, and our society as a whole rest. Breaking the taboo requires unwavering determination. It did for Naomi. It does for most of us. Our fear is that we will have to give up something we crave—the possibility of love. But I am here to tell you that this is not true and that by breaking the taboo, we may instead recover that which we have lost: our power.

Money Is Power

> "Only the powerless live in a money culture and know nothing about money."—PHYLLIS CHESLER

Here we get to what could be the very core of our problems with money. In simple practical terms, money is nothing more than paper and metal we use to purchase products and services, no different from beads, furs, or other wampum our ancestors used to pay for goods. Yet most of us recognize that money is far more than a means of exchange. Even if we perceive it metaphorically as freedom, security, love, or happiness, the profound truth that women, in particular, need to understand is: Money means power. As Phyllis Chesler wrote in *Women, Money and Power*: "Money is a power sacred to most men and foreign to most women."

Money, in and of itself, does not give us power. It is merely a tool, and like many other tools, it does us no good unless we know how to use it. My first marriage is a prime example. I had the money, but my husband had the power. He made the decisions. Money bestows power by giving us choices. Money gives us the freedom and the resources to make choices based on who we are and what we want, not on what someone else expects or society dictates. *No matter how much money a woman has, unless she is knowledgeable and responsible for it, she can never fully tap the power money holds.* It is our understanding of how money works and our ability to manage it autonomously that empower us.

"Control is where the real action is," Paula Nelson writes in *The Joy of Money*, adding, "and the fun."

But before we can experience the fun, we must break the taboos. Everyone, whether man or woman, has suffered from its effects. By taking financial control, women are not competing with or diminishing men in any way. Quite the contrary. A financially independent woman is the final emancipation for both sexes. Historically, men have always had permission to be powerful. But with the permission came the pressure. Men were obliged to achieve worldly and financial success. Their families counted upon them for it, and the world judged them by it. It was a heavy burden to bear. And they bore that yoke alone. But as women take charge of their money, all that will begin to change. The burden of success will be lifted from men, just as the mantle of subjugation will be lifted from women. Everyone will then be freer to make satisfying personal choices. Men and women can work together, interdependently, as equals and partners, rather than in some sort of culturally prescribed symbiosis. We owe it to ourselves and our children. None of us should ever have to tolerate harassment from a boss or abuse from a spouse. We should never have to suffer any sort of indignation, exploitation, or financial hardship. Nor should we ever have to sacrifice self-determination for future security.

"We are doing it for ourselves," Linda Pei, founder of the Women's Equity Mutual Fund, told me. "In the process, we can make the world a lot better."

How do we break the taboo? How do we silence the warning voices within us? To do so requires courage, make no mistake. Financial enlightenment demands far more from us than picking up a few tidbits of information or plunking down a few dollars for stock. Getting smart with money, for most women, constitutes a rite of passage. It is a transformational experience, a hero's—no, a heroine's—journey.

The Heroine's Journey to Financial Independence

The purpose of all heroes', or heroines', journeys, according to the late mythologist Joseph Campbell, is the transformation of consciousness. "You have been thinking one way," he explains. "Now you have to think a different way."

Isn't that what happens when we start taking charge of our finances? We've been thinking one way ("I feel so stupid"); now we have to think another ("I am capable and responsible"). We are called upon to shed our dependency and ignorance, our antiquated beliefs and societal taboos, anything that's kept us imprisoned in the past. It is "a process of throwing off the old and coming into the new," says Campbell. Particularly interesting is his observation that, so often, the journey begins with defiance. The hero does something she is not supposed to do.

"Life really begins with the act of disobedience," Campbell once explained. Take the biblical story of Eve who ate the apple. "Now God must have known very well that man was going to eat the forbidden fruit," he explains. "But it was by doing this that man became the initiator of his own life."

In our case, the forbidden fruit is money. To become the initiators of our own lives, we must disobey the cultural prohibitions against our achieving financial independence. Such bravado requires courage—

courage to venture beyond the boundaries of what is safe and known, to challenge the taboos, to feel the foreboding, and to keep on going. The opposite of courage is not the absence of fear. It is automatic conformity.

The women who share their stories throughout this book are heroines in the true sense of the word. From them, I finally grasped how people who become smart with money are able to muster up the courage to do so. Actually, I sensed what they did long before I fully understood it. And I began following in their footsteps long before I could articulate exactly what I was doing.

It wasn't until I was asked to speak at a forum on women and money for a local college that I figured out what the process of becoming smart with money was all about. In preparing for my speech, I reread my interviews with smart women and pondered what I had learned. Though their experiences were diverse, these women shared surprising similarities. As I studied the transcripts and thought about my own experience, I became aware of seven themes that ran through their stories like seven common threads woven through a collection of complicated tapestries. These themes, I began to see, were actually a series of recognitions or insights every woman had. These insights, sometimes on the order of epiphanies, ran counter to the myths and beliefs most of us have about money. I call these insights *realizations*. Every woman I spoke to had come to each of these seven realizations one way or another.

I found these realizations incredibly powerful, remarkably illuminating, like mysteries revealed, truths unveiled. I saw that incorporating them into my thinking was what had enabled me finally to start taking financial responsibility for myself. What's more, I recognized that these seven realizations, when combined, form a process. In other words, they become the stepping-stones that mark our way in the heroine's journey, each taking us one step closer to getting smart with money.

Getting Smart Is a Two-Part Process

Though money knows no gender, my research confirmed my conviction that the path to financial enlightenment can be very different for women than for men. Certainly, many men have emotional blocks around money. But generally speaking, women, as we've seen, struggle with very different, deeply ingrained issues that are specifically related to growing up female. For women to achieve financial self-sufficiency, I believe we must follow a two-pronged process. In other words, we have two tasks we must accomplish in order to reach our goal: I call these two tasks the *outer work* and the *inner work*. The outer work tackles practical matters and deals with factual information; the inner work explores the psychological realm and focuses on emotional awareness. *It is the inner work of transforming our beliefs and attitudes combined with the outer work of absorbing hard-nosed facts that ensures our success.* That is why, for many of us, reading an investment book isn't enough. Financial proficiency occurs when rational data is coupled with personal insight, when we develop our financial skills while transcending our personal limitations.

I once spoke to psychologist Carol Sirulnick, who explained it like this: "My experience is that women will take classes, read books, but they don't find out why it is so hard for them to make decisions. And the reason is generally emotional. If you don't do the emotional work, you have a hard time making financial decisions."

Stockbroker Ellen Stromberg similarly observed: "Fifteen years ago, no one thought that there might be more to investing than studying companies. But it's become clear that emotions are important, especially for women. We women take in so many messages and fears from society and family, so many unwritten rules that shape our feelings about money. Understanding these messages can make it easier to understand financial decisions."

But confronting these emotions can be a formidable challenge, like sitting naked in front of a mirror. Granted that for some women, examining finances is no big deal. But for many of us, it is a very uncomfortable experience. We are forced to see what we've been trying to hide and would rather ignore. Like corks long held under water, a whole range of feelings may rush to the surface: nervousness, apprehension, grief, insecurity, shame, guilt, or inadequacy. We begin to see our own barriers, the way we've been socialized, decisions we've made that didn't serve us. We come face-to-face with our deepest fears of becoming a bag lady, getting old, being alone. All kinds of questions arise. What if it's too late? What if I can't learn this? What if I make the same mistakes again?

No matter how successful or how smart women may have become, so many who are afflicted with self-doubt and a deep sense of vulnerability. After all, we are about to do something we weren't trained, expected, or even permitted to do.

Transforming our self-doubt to self-reliance, our vulnerability to determination, and our ignorance to understanding is, as I have said, a two-part process. The realizations that follow will serve as your road map for this journey. The first three realizations will guide you through the inner work. The next three focus primarily on the outer work. By witnessing how other women attained these realizations, and how they put the realizations into action, I hope you will come to see, as I have, that there is nothing mysterious about money. Any woman can become as financially astute as men are claimed to be. And if you still have doubts, keep holding the thought: that maybe, just maybe, you can too.

Part Two

• •

THE PROCESS

The following chapters describe a series of "ahas," —realizations that jolted women out of their financial lethargy. In part, these are psychological states. Yet they are also practical steps. When combined, these realizations form a map and a mind-set.

I call them the **Seven Realizations of Financial Enlightenment**. In this part, we will consider the first six:

1. No one will do this for me.
2. Learning follows a curve.
3. All the answers aren't out there.
4. There are no secrets.
5. Risk is not a synonym for loss.
6. I don't have to do this alone.

The Inner Work of Wealth Checklist

• • • • • • • • • • • • • • •

The next three chapters are devoted to what I call the Inner Work of Wealth. Some of you, anxious to get to the nitty-gritty, the practical nuts and bolts, may be wondering: Do *I* really need to engage in self-reflection? Is the inner work really necessary in *my* situation? Before you dismiss it, try filling out the checklist below. Do any of these apply to you?

☐ 1. I am not doing anything to create wealth, even though I know I should.
☐ 2. I've done a little bit, not nearly enough, yet I can't get going.
☐ 3. I am constantly making excuses to justify my inactivity.
☐ 4. I am reluctant to seek outside financial guidance.
☐ 5. I feel that money is bad, wealth is off limits, and financial success is for other people.
☐ 6. I constantly overspend.
☐ 7. I am always struggling to make ends meet, no matter how much money I make.
☐ 8. I refuse to worry about money or my retirement.
☐ 9. I have a family history of money problems.
☐ 10. I grew up in poverty and can't seem to break the cycle.
☐ 11. I was raised to believe someone else would take care of me financially.
☐ 12. I have little or no confidence in my ability to handle money.

If you have checked even one of these statements, you would be well advised to undertake the inner work suggested in the following three chapters. The outer work becomes infinitely easier, and far more successful, when you are able to identify and overcome internal blocks.

• • • • • • • • • • • • • • •

Chapter Three

• •

Realization #1:
No One Will Do This for Me

*When the heart weeps for what it has lost,
the spirit laughs for what it has found.*
—SUFI APHORISM

At first I couldn't put my finger on it. Early in the course of my interviews with women who successfully managed their money, I noticed that
there was something markedly different about their attitudes. What was
it? Self-reliance? Resiliency? Autonomy? All those words applied, but I
sensed something more. Eventually it dawned on me. At some point in our
conversations, each woman would describe a moment when she realized,
with stunning clarity: *"Prince Charming isn't coming. I have to do this
myself."*

Even if they didn't use those exact words, all had a remarkably similar
realization.

"I always made good money. But I didn't understand I needed to save
it," Meredith told me. Meredith was a vibrant professional woman in her
mid-thirties, with cascading blond hair and a disarming warm smile. "I
thought Prince Charming was going to ride in on his white horse, swoop
down and scoop me up, and support me through my retirement, so I could
spend what I earned and didn't have to save."

"What changed that?" I asked.

"After Max and I split up, it just hit me," she recalled. "I realized this fantasy was not a reality. I'd better start being one hundred percent responsible. I couldn't sit around waiting for Mr. Right to make me rich. *I had to do it myself.*"

Sometimes, this first realization hits with the force of an oncoming train; other times, it comes as a quiet awakening. For some women, the realization didn't occur until they were middle-aged or older. For others, the insight emerged much earlier; in some instances, as early as childhood.

"I was twelve years old," recalled one woman who had grown up in poverty. "It was like an epiphany, a glimpse of enlightenment. I suddenly understood that I didn't have to live like my parents, that I was in charge of my own life, I was the mistress of my own ship. I'll never forget it. It was an amazing experience for a seventh grader."

For every single woman, young or old, the recognition was far more than a cerebral experience. It was a visceral sensation, an absolute knowing, deep in their gut: *No one will do this for me.*

The Turning Point

Coming to this realization was a defining moment, a turning point in each woman's financial life. In this moment she transferred the authority for her life from the external world to herself. Virtually every smart woman I interviewed spoke of this realization as an awakening that led to action.

Please note: "Mr. Right" or "Prince Charming" need not be a man, or even a person. Our "prince" could be an ideal job, an insurance settlement, the lottery jackpot, or just an amorphous "something"—anything that we fantasize will save us financially. To become genuinely smart with money, we must get to the point where we can say with total conviction, *I can do it myself.* It doesn't matter if we are single, married, or living with a partner. Until we cast off our dependency and know with every fiber of our being that the quality of our future hinges on our assuming responsibility, we will never fully take charge of our finances. We'll never really believe we can do it ourselves—not as long as even a tiny part of us is waiting for, hoping, expecting someone (or something outside ourselves) to do it for us.

I remember an unexpectedly revealing interview for one of my newspaper columns with Polly Bergen, an acclaimed actress who became an auspicious businesswoman. She told me how she turned a $15,000 investment into a $6 million cosmetics company, Oil of the Turtle. "Then, when it became a million-dollar business," she said, "I thought, Jesus, I am not smart enough to run this company." So she hired a man, gave him her big office, an enormous salary, and complete control. "I stepped across the hall and paid myself $25,000."

The next year, when the company lost $950,000, she fired him, hired another man, and continued to lose money. "I still kept thinking a man's smarter. He can do it better," she said.

Eventually she sold the company at a loss. At the same time, she got a divorce. She took her divorce settlement of $140,000 and turned it into $4 million by investing in real estate. She remarried and, with her husband, started a jewelry company. This time, her husband invested the profits in the stock market and lost everything. Again, she was forced to sell the business at a loss.

Finally Polly woke up. "Since I was eighteen, I earned six figures, sometimes seven. But I'd give my power away, abdicate responsibility. As long as there is no man around, I can make millions. But as soon as there is a man, I turn it over to him. I am starting to realize I am smart. If I trust myself, do what I know is right, ninety percent of the time I am right on target."

Polly's story underscores a fundamental truth: Women who attempt to take charge while awaiting Prince Charming are rarely successful. Harboring a rescue fantasy while trying to manage money is like driving a car with watered-down gas. We're not going to get very far. Our efforts get diluted. Our intentions lose their potency. Try as we may, taking responsibility remains a struggle, a pretense, or a partial undertaking. I have observed this phenomenon in interviews with other women, but even more, I know this from my own experience.

When I received my second tax bill, the one for over $600,000, I vividly remember thinking that for the first time in my life, I had no backup. The

IRS was threatening to take away my trust fund. My father refused to bail me out. My ex-husband wouldn't help. And the lawyers held out little hope. There wasn't a man in sight who would save me. There was no escaping the truth. I couldn't keep running away. I had to get serious and do something, not just go through the motions. That realization, though torturous, was also transforming.

Gradually, as I renewed my efforts to get smart about money, this time in earnest, I became aware that a new truth was putting forth shoots where the old one had been uprooted. The aching awareness that "no one is there for me" slowly evolved into a powerful recognition: "I can do it. I am there for me." But that discovery came much later. First I had to come to grips with the fact that Prince Charming wasn't coming.

The Prince Charming Myth

Dispelling the myth that someday our prince will come is the most important financial decision we will ever make. Unfortunately, it's a decision countless women have yet to reach. In a survey of 23,000 readers, *Ms.* magazine found that the majority of respondents grew up with the expectation that someone else, usually a man, probably a husband, would do the financial planning in their lives.

"I meet a lot of women because I lecture around the country," says Colette Dowling, author of *The Cinderella Complex*, the 1970s bestseller about women's dependency needs. "It concerns me in a very fundamental way that there are so many women who really don't want to take responsibility for themselves, who still think 'I am doing this until the next man comes along.'"

Chris Hayes, director of the National Center for Women and Retirement Research (NCWRR), agrees. "Despite the women's movement, there is a large percentage of women who want very much to be taken care of. This has surprised us no end in our research."

It may have been a surprise to him. But it's not a bit surprising to most of us. I don't think there was a woman I talked to who didn't refer to a white knight, a Prince Charming, a savior of some sort. Even if women didn't adhere to the myth, they were aware of its presence. This is a collective secret, a silent understanding we women share.

As one woman told me, "I used to sit down with girlfriends whose financial lives were a mess, and my first line to them was: 'What are you going to do if Prince Charming doesn't come? How are you going to take care of yourself?' A lot of my friends won't buy a home unless there is a man in their life. And they aren't doing anything about retirement."

The rescue myth has been so tightly woven into our social conditioning, I sometimes wonder if it hasn't worked its way into our genetic code. As John Bradshaw told *Lear's* magazine: "The most common form of magic that I find dominating women's lives is the notion of waiting—the idea that if you just wait long enough, something good will happen." Even among the most self-reliant women I interviewed, so many had to fight hard to liberate themselves from this beguiling fiction. "Did you ever think a man was going to come along and take care of you?" I began asking successful investors. Their answers were incredibly similar.

"Absolutely. Absolutely," exclaimed Marion, a handsome woman in her fifties. "Until he didn't." She laughed at her admission. Marion runs a successful consulting firm, makes good money, and recently married an equally successful man. But it wasn't always that way. "I spent forty years of my life sitting around waiting for the man to come along and do all this for me. My mother brainwashed me. She told me, 'You live at home until you marry. Then Prince Charming comes, and you live happily ever after.'"

"Isn't that part of our makeup as females?" Meredith said, chuckling, as we discussed this "rescue myth" phenomenon. "Aren't we all trained that way from birth? I think all women have the same conversation about money, at least the women I know. 'Someone else will do it.'"

Indeed, Meredith, like Marion and countless others, had been brainwashed with these beliefs. "My father thought it was bad for a woman to know more than a man about money," Meredith explained. "He was afraid that if I was too intelligent, I'd never have a husband."

When it comes to money, I see this as one of the major differences between men and women. Men may speak wistfully of being rescued. They may resist taking responsibility, may even fantasize about winning the lottery or marrying an heiress. But they don't regard it as their birthright. I've yet to hear a man, young or old, say he's waiting around for his princess before he gets serious about his portfolio.

"Prince Charming is the most damaging myth that has been perpetuated in my generation," railed a woman in her late sixties. But it's not just older women who are waiting for the next man to come along. Many in their twenties operate with the same agenda.

"We expected to find that younger women would see their mothers' mistakes and protect themselves," says Chris Hayes of NCWRR. "What we're finding is that younger women are so busy trying to succeed, juggling family, career, and marriage, that they are not looking out for themselves financially."

A large-scale study on women and divorce conducted by NCWRR documented that younger women were as negligent about money as older women. Many younger women may not have been brought up to rely on a man, but they are simply overburdened with responsibilities. Their negligence is, in part, easily masked by the fact that they are making money. Still others see their mothers and sisters worn out from trying to manage a career and a family, and they say to themselves, "I don't want this. It's too exhausting." Oftentimes these women look for a husband to lighten the load.

For numerous women, regardless of age, their sense of self-worth and feelings of being lovable are intertwined with finding a man to take care of them. "There is something so exciting about someone taking care of my credit cards," a woman admitted when talking about her boyfriend. "I get to be like a little girl being taken care of. Someone taking care of my bills means he cares about me."

When the Prince Takes a Powder

Indeed, there is something seductive and compelling about curling up under someone else's economic wing. When someone shoulders our financial burdens, we feel loved and provided for. This is the role model for relationships most of us grew up with. We saw it in our families. We watched it on television. We read about it in the storybooks. Ozzie took care of Harriet. The dashing prince rescued the helpless damsel. While the man went out into the world to make a buck or slay the dragon, a woman didn't have to do a thing (other than look beautiful) to live happily ever after. The passive princess became our prototype. She set the standard for finding love.

"I bought into this whole myth," Renee, now a financial counselor, told me. "You married the right man. He took care of you. I always pictured it that way. My mother never worked. My mother's mother didn't work. There wasn't a family member who worked except my maiden aunt—and there were a lot of jokes made about her. In our family, there was something wrong with the husband if he couldn't support you, or something wrong with you if you didn't get married."

As expected, Renee married young and her husband took care of everything. But all that changed when her marriage fell apart. "It was shattering," she recalled. "I felt I wasn't lovable. Other women got their knight, but I was going to be like my maiden aunt. I thought there was something intrinsically wrong with me."

It's scary to think of how many of us have fallen into the same self-deprecating trap, convinced that "I am no good without a man."

What's even scarier is the number of women who have been soothed into a kind of financial stupor, believing they've found their prince because they've married someone who takes care of everything. When they abdicate financial responsibility to the man in their life, they take perhaps the greatest financial risk a woman could take today, for two reasons.

First of all, relatively few marriages last anymore. As declared in the *New York Times*, "Divorce is becoming a mid-life phenomenon."

"Once upon a time [women] went into the wife business," observed former *New York Times* columnist Anna Quindlen. These women relied on their homemaking skills and their husbands' good fortune to provide future security. But their husbands had different ideas. Consequently, notes Quindlen, "There are those who say that the housewife has gone the way of the tuna casserole."

For many housewives, splintered marriages create shattered lives. Divorce is the major cause of poverty among women, said the New York State Assembly Task Force on Women's Issues. Studies show that when a woman divorces, her net worth plummets 43 percent. (In contrast, a man's jumps 23 percent.) Five years later, few have regained their former status. Tragically, single mothers have become the fastest-growing segment of the homeless population.

Even if the marriage survives, the husband often doesn't. Most women outlive their spouses by at least seven years. According to *Working Woman* magazine, our longevity can have chilling consequences. "Roughly 80 percent of the widows now living in poverty were not poor before their husbands' death," the magazine reports.

Whatever the reason—divorce, death, or deliberate decision—the vast majority of us, at least 90 percent, will spend some part of our life alone and thus be responsible for our own finances. That part typically comes when we are older. Not surprisingly, a 1990 issue of *Family Circle* magazine declared, "The '90s will be a grim time for older women." Think about these facts:

- 48 percent of all women will be widowed: their average age, 56.
- 36 percent will divorce: their average age, 46.
- 6 percent will remain single.

We can, of course, toss off these figures as "just statistics," reassuring ourselves "it won't happen to me," but such self-deception can be exceedingly dangerous. It leaves us helplessly unprepared should our prince/spouse depart. I remember reading about Joan Rivers, the highly successful talk show host and comedienne, who admitted to a newspaper reporter that when her husband died she didn't even know the name of her bank. (Years later, in an interview with *Working Woman*, a wiser Rivers declared: "Trust no one with your money, because no one is smarter than you when it comes to your money. Well, they may be smarter, but you care more.")

I spoke with a woman whose experiences as an administrator for an investment firm literally scared her into taking charge of her money.

"I worked with a lot of doctors," she told me. "If I wanted to know about their finances, I'd ask their office managers or CPAs. I never asked their wives. In two different instances, a doctor died and the wife had no idea where the money was. The wives ended up calling me. I would pull a financial statement and start walking them through it. I'd tell them who to talk to and what to ask and where to look for information.

"That these women could be in this position terrified me. I still had this myth that the wife of a doctor had no problems. Yet in both of these cases, when I pulled the financial statements, I saw the husband had invested totally inappropriately. Most of their money was in tax shelters. There was nothing their wives could get hold of. That really made me understand that no one out there is going to help you. All those myths, have a man take care of you, were shot from under me."

The Reality Beyond the Myth

Those myths *should* be shot out from all of us—the sooner the better. No one today can afford to be financially ignorant. We reside in a country that has no national health insurance, hardly any subsidized child care or elder care, shrinking social security payments, no job security, and inadequate pensions. Compared to men, women earn less, save less, have higher rates of disability, and drop out of the workforce more often, losing precious benefits. We live longer, so what we have must last longer. Too often, we have only ourselves to fall back on.

"Women need to realize that no one is going to take care of them," Chris Hayes of NCWRR says bluntly. "The government isn't going to be there. Their husbands may not be. Or even their families. Their best friend in terms of their financial security is themselves."

The Myth, Not the Man, Has to Go

Which is not to say that we have to relinquish our relationships in order to assume financial responsibility. Stockbroker Esther Berger, author of *Money Smart: Secrets Women Need to Know About Money*, tells the story of a female reporter from a major newspaper who came to her house to interview her. Esther's husband and two young sons were also there. When the interview ended, the reporter said earnestly, "Esther, I pictured you very differently. I figured you'd be this real aggressive hard-nosed type. And here are your kids running around asking for cookies."

Esther understood immediately why the woman said this. "Society just assumes someone taking financial responsibility can't have a husband and children," she explained. This assumption is part of the taboo. But it's a lie. The truth is, *we can give up the myth without giving up the man*. Just because a woman is self-sufficient doesn't mean she must be self-contained, or celibate.

Psychologists tell us that when a woman becomes financially independent, she gains self-assurance and peace of mind, and her relationships become healthier and more mature. As psychotherapist Annette Lieberman points out in *Unbalanced Accounts*, women who are good with money enjoy better sex lives. "Those who take charge of their money," she writes, "develop the same qualities people need to enjoy sex: higher self-esteem, a sense of mastery, confidence, and permission to enjoy pleasure."

Many of the women I interviewed were quite happily married or in satisfying relationships. In fact, it's precisely because I took financial control that *I* am too. Cal's office was right across the hall from mine, but in three years, we had barely said more than hello as we passed in the hallway. When I decided to get serious about money, one of the things I did was talk to everyone I met who knew about investing. I had heard that Cal made his living in the stock market. One day, I poked my head into his office. "You do investing, don't you?" I asked him. He smiled and nodded. "I'm trying to get a handle on the subject," I explained. "Can I take you out for lunch someday and pick your brain?"

The next day, we went to a nearby Chinese restaurant. I briefly described my situation, and he generously shared his expertise. After that we met regularly. I'd tell him what I was learning, he'd give me feedback, and we'd bounce ideas around. He quickly became my mentor. He also became a good friend. A year later, he became my husband.

A number of the financially savvy women I interviewed were married to equally savvy men. Others had partners who were their polar opposites, with no money, no financial skills, or no interest in the subject. If, as Freud said, there are no coincidences, I wondered if these women were trying to eliminate any financial cushions so they'd be forced to take charge. Several women spoke of this quite candidly.

"My husband could care less about this stuff," a woman told me. "I look at it as an advantage. I know if my husband were different, I wouldn't do anything. I know me. I'd stay where I was comfortable. I wouldn't do it myself otherwise. I wouldn't push myself."

Most women, in fact, discover they like taking charge, being part of the action. Even if they don't run the show, they feel infinitely more secure and self-confident when they understand what is going on behind the scenes and know enough to make informed financial decisions or keep tabs on the people who are making those decisions for them.

Renouncing the Prince

Meredith, thinking it was Prince Charming galloping in on his white horse, gladly let her husband take the financial reins. Only now does she realize that while she welcomed her husband's control, part of her was "scared to death."

"I was at his mercy," she recalled, "and it drove me batty. I had no understanding of money. I didn't understand about the compounding effect of interest and earnings on money, or even the basic nuts and bolts." She hesitated, apparently reflecting on that early marriage. "To not have any of the fundamentals makes you feel so powerless."

Upon her divorce, Meredith finally took action, or as she put it, "I carved out my own stake." She opened a bank account and started setting aside a certain amount of cash in savings. As she told me proudly, "I became very active in managing my money."

It was the best thing that could have happened to her, she readily admits. "I know that having the willingness to be responsible, knowing where your money is, how you spend it, gives us tremendous personal power."

How do we do what Meredith did? How do those of us still clinging to the fantasy finally let go? To find our answer, let's look at how other women did it. For some, renouncing the myth was easy, especially if they grew up with the unquestionable advantage of supportive parents.

"I used to watch my father chart stock prices when I was nine and ten years old," one woman reminisced. "He was always clear we had to manage our available cash. So I grew up knowing I had to manage money, and I grew up knowing there was a stock market."

For others, their self-reliance was born of deep wounds suffered in childhood. A mother who died young. A father who beat them. One parent was an alcoholic. Another was just never around. These women grew up amid deprivation and abuse.

"I never expected a man to take care of me," said Julie, a business-woman who by age forty had made enough money in the sale of her com-pany to retire and live off her investments. "My father was an alcoholic. I don't recall us ever having any money to spend. I started baby-sitting when I was twelve years old. I decided if there was no money in the house, I would make it myself. I learned not to rely on my parents. I learned not to rely on anyone. I have no idea how I would have turned out if I had grown up in a family with money."

Indeed, those raised in a wealthy family, often cushioned from life's blows, frequently have a harder time taking the financial reins.

But regardless of their background, the majority of women I inter-viewed pointed to a crisis as their impetus for change. Maybe it's part of our human nature, or a by-product of the taboo against female self-reliance. The truth is, most women don't become fiscally responsible un-til they are pushed to do so. Studies show that women who face a job loss or a failed marriage are the most likely to look out for themselves financially.

As I pointed out in the Introduction, and will continue to note throughout, if there is one lesson to be learned from this book, it is this: Don't wait for a crisis to end your inertia. Your awakening need not be dra-matic, traumatic, or painful. You can disconnect from the myth without devastating your life. Remember, all it takes is a decision. Renouncing Prince Charming is a conscious and constant choice.

"You have to make a decision to be powerful," one woman declared. "It's like refusing to let some bully on the block knock you down. You can be a victim and wait for someone to make it okay, or you can do it yourself."

I remember asking Marion, whose mother told her explicitly that

Prince Charming would be coming, how she changed that notion. It took a lot of soul searching, she acknowledged. "I realized I needed to look at my experiences as being valid, instead of my beliefs," she said thoughtfully. "My *experience* had been that men basically are not going to take care of you. You have to learn to take care of yourself. But my *beliefs* were that there has to be someone that will come rescue me, and I've just chosen the wrong people. But no one rescued me, and I spent a lot of time waiting. I finally realized my beliefs were really holding me back."

Patricia, another woman I interviewed, who believed financial success would scare off a man, took a more analytical approach. She said everything changed when she sat down and did a financial plan, calculating her assets, liabilities, and retirement needs. "When I did the plan, I saw that even if I don't get married, I can have a decent lifestyle as long as I continue saving money," she explained. "I had this tremendous anxiety, thinking there will never be enough, that this picture is never going to be bright unless I have a partner. Now I know I don't have to have a partner."

The realization came as a tremendous relief. "I don't want to tie in the need for a partner with money," she said. "Not having to worry about money can enhance a relationship. But I don't want to rely on a man for money. I don't want to look at him as a retirement plan."

The Fallout

For many of us, however, this first realization is far from reassuring. Acknowledging the fact that our prince isn't coming can be as unsettling as a child finding out there is no Santa Claus, a disappointing, if not agonizing, experience. The awareness may hit us like whiplash, painfully shredding the whole fabric of our assumptions, leaving us raw with anger, anguish, and fear. We're angry at the man for not being there, at the world for telling us he will be, and at our own gullibility for believing this baloney. We're aching from the loss of our illusions and for the death of our dreams. And we're terrified of navigating the unknown all by ourselves.

"It was the bursting of a bubble," recalled Meredith, referring to her divorce. "It was terrifying, really. To realize that for the rest of my life I'd have to take care of myself financially. I didn't have a clue how to do it. I felt very lost, with no idea where to begin. I had no skills, no role models." For a long time, she said, she was not only scared, she was mad.

"I was furious. I felt I should have had this explained to me when I was twenty, not thirty-six. I felt way behind in terms of years. And I had an eighteen-month-old baby. There was a part of me—the female who grew up thinking a man would take care of me—that was incensed."

Countless women I've talked to have told me how angry they were when they realized no man, nor any twist of fate, would rescue them. Anger is a normal part of the letting-go process. And for good reason. While anger can be debilitating, it can also be galvanizing. As one woman declared, "I think you need a little bit of anger. It's a healthy anger. You have to refuse to settle. You have to refuse to be mediocre. You simply say, 'I'm mad as hell, and I'm not going to take it anymore.'"

No matter how we come to the realization that Prince Charming isn't coming, no matter how it may hurt, it is the awareness that gets us going and sets us free. But letting this myth go may not happen overnight. Nor should we deny this mind-set exists. That which we ignore we empower.

Letting Go

Meredith is now a successful corporate trainer doing a beautiful job of coming to grips with her finances. During our interview, I asked her, "Is there a part of you that still wants Prince Charming?" Her response echoed what many others told me.

"It's still there," she admitted, slightly embarrassed. "The belief still comes up. I just have to recognize that it's a conversation in my head and remember it's not a reality. I'm dating this guy now who makes a couple hundred grand a year and has a lot of disposable income. At first I thought, Whew." She laughed at her reaction. "Immediately I stopped myself. 'Wrong. Wrong thinking. Don't think this.'" She sighed. "It's an old belief that dies hard."

It's an old belief that dies hard. So many others I interviewed said the same thing. These were powerful, competent women who had vowed to take control, were doing a good job managing their money, and were enjoying the responsibility. Yet they still had moments when they wished to be rescued. The Prince Charming myth is tenacious and insidious. Even when we have deliberately cast it aside, its lingering appeal may never go away. The archetype remains forever an integral part of our collective unconscious. Allowing the myth to die a natural death may be an erratic process, a roller-coaster ride of ups and downs. It was for me. I found myself simultaneously trying to bury it while yearning to resurrect it.

"Part of me just wants to do nothing. Let someone else take care of me," I wrote in my journal during a bout with my tax bills. "I feel so polarized. Part of me is driven. The other part is paralyzed. One part knows I'm capable. The other is terrified I'm not. One part is ready to do something. The other part just wants to stay in bed."

Then I met Cal. It was so tempting to see him as my savior. But by this time my determination to be smart was stronger than my desire to be saved. (How often, when we make a commitment, do we find our resolve being tested?) I realized that until I could take care of myself, I would never have a healthy relationship. I now needed to become like the kind of man I had been looking for.

Moving On

There is no one right way to get to that point where we finally say to ourselves, with total certainty, "I know Prince Charming isn't coming. I *have* to do it myself. I *can* do it myself. I *want* to do it myself." However, if I had to give a formula for coming to this realization, it would consist of the following three steps:

- First, we need to be open to the possibility: *What if Prince Charming never comes?* (Or, for those who think they've found their prince: *What if he leaves?*)
- Second, we need to recognize the truth: *No one will do this for me.*
- Third, we need to give ourselves a nudge: *Maybe, just maybe, I can do this for myself.*

The decision to stop relying on others and take charge of our money is one we may need to make over and over again. Whenever we find ourselves thinking: "Someday my prince will come," we must change the words to: "I can do it. I am there for me." Even then, as the myth dissolves, our apprehension may not instantly follow suit.

Sometimes, waving good-bye to Prince Charming can be a lonely experience, as if we're lost in the middle of a dark forest. We may feel apprehensive, insecure, and all alone, wondering, What do I do now? If you find yourself at all reluctant to release the myth or are experiencing a kind of existential angst at doing so, then keep reading. The realizations that follow will explain exactly how to build a solid base on which we can rest our ladder—the one we'll use to climb up and over our financial hurdles. The first rung of that ladder is Realization #2.

••• CHAPTER THREE RECAPPED •••

Realization: We will never become truly smart about money, no matter how hard we try, until we explicitly decide: *No one is going to take care of my money for me; that responsibility falls on my shoulders.* This declaration is the beginning of the inner work and the quintessential step in the entire process.

To Do

1. Observe your thoughts as you read this book. Do you detect a little voice saying things like: "I don't have time for this," or "Sure, it's easy for her to talk, she's got money," or "Maybe, just maybe, someone *will* come along and do this for me." Those thoughts may be fleeting, or barely audible, but they're surprisingly powerful. Keep countering those negative voices with: *"I can do this. I will do this. I want to do this."* Let these words be your daily mantra, even if you don't completely believe them at first.

2. If you're married (or about to be), this book is required reading: *What Every Woman Should Know About Her Husband's Money*, by Shelby White (Random House, 1992).

3. A revealing exercise: Call Social Security (800-772-1213) and ask for an estimate of your retirement benefits. It will be immediately apparent that Uncle Sam is no Prince Charming.

(The purpose of the following suggestions is to build a solid foundation for future investing. If you have already done these, you're ahead of the game!)

4. Set up a plan to pay off your debts. If you have any unmortgaged debts, particularly unpaid credit card bills, figure out how you can pay them off. The interest you're paying on credit card debt is outrageous. Talk to the Consumer Credit Counselors (800-200-6444), write to the National Center for Financial Education (P.O. Box 34070, San Diego, CA 92163), contact the National Center for Women and Retirement Research (Long Island University, Southampton, N.Y. 11968), or order *The Financial Recovery Workbook* by Karen McCall (800-722-0110).

5. Set up a forced savings plan. Adequate savings for emergencies must be in place before you invest. Make it easy for yourself. Arrange to have your bank automatically transfer a certain amount of money every month from your checking account to a savings account or money market account. How much? Whatever you can afford. Ten percent of your income is the ideal, but even $10 a month is fine. (If you do not have your own bank account, only a joint one with your husband, open an account in your name *today*.)

6. Set up a tax-deferred retirement plan if you don't already have one. How? Talk to your accountant or your employer. If you have one, are you contributing the maximum allowed, or that you can afford, to this plan every year? Do you know what's in it and how it's doing? If you don't know, find out. Again, consult an accountant or your employer.

• •

Realization #2:
Learning Follows a Curve

> *There are no shortcuts in the journey ahead, nor is*
> *there a turning back. . . . Development must be*
> *allowed to take its proper course.*
> —*I Ching*

For a long time, my interviews with smart women were unsettling ordeals. Listening to them talk about money, I'd feel like an illiterate at a Mensa meeting. Within moments, I'd be overcome with awe (How do they know all this stuff?), envy (I wish I were that smart . . .), and massive self-doubt (. . . but I never will be). I knew there was no way I'd ever achieve their expertise. Then I interviewed a woman who had struggled much as I had to decipher her finances.

"You're so knowledgeable," I blurted out. "I can't imagine ever being like that."

"Well," she said matter-of-factly, "you're getting me at the tail end of a very long learning curve."

Her offhand remark stuck with me for days. I began to hear other women express similar sentiments. As I mulled over what these women were saying, I began to realize why I had been having such a hard time mastering money. It wasn't that I was incapable. I just hadn't understood that learning about money is like learning about anything else. *And the learning follows a curve.* It takes time. I began to realize I wasn't permanently impaired, just temporarily disadvantaged—a stranger in a strange land.

The Land of the Financially Fluent

When we enter the investment world, it's like stepping into a foreign country. We can no longer live solely as consumers but must adapt to the ways of the wealth builders. Newcomers can feel like strangers, and simple decisions can boggle the mind. What do we do? Where do we invest? Is the stock market the only option? How do we decide? It's so easy for beginners to get bewildered. The investment world has its own rules, customs, and often indecipherable vocabulary.

Case in point: Alan Greenspan, chairman of the Federal Reserve, once told a group of reporters: "If I seem unduly clear to you, you must have misunderstood what I said."

"It's a vocabulary to keep people out!" financial consultant Joyce Linker says emphatically. "You know, every profession has a vocabulary, and I think it's designed to keep the nonprofessionals out. It makes it mysterious. Once you learn the vocabulary, you realize it's really common sense."

Indeed, common sense and some basic knowledge is all we really need to become financially fluent. Look at it this way. There are only five places to invest money: *stock, bonds, real estate, commodities,* and *cash or cash equivalents.* Five categories, or, in "brokerese," five asset classes.

If you're unfamiliar with these categories, here is a very brief, simple explanation:

- *Stock* is ownership in a company. When you buy a hundred shares of IBM, you become a partial, albeit small, owner of the giant computer firm. If the value of your stock goes up, you make money. If the price of the stock goes down, you lose money.
- A *bond* is an IOU. When you buy a bond, the issuer of that bond, normally a corporation, a government or its agency, promises to

pay you back in full, plus interest, by a certain date. Bonds also fluctuate, but if you hold the bond until it matures, and if the borrower remains solvent, your initial investment will be returned. (Bonds, which offer steady income, less risk, but no growth, are considered conservative investments.)

- *Cash equivalents*, such as money market funds, certificates of deposits, and short-term treasury bills, pay minimal interest, are highly liquid (easily converted to cash), and guarantee a full return. Cash equivalents won't make you wealthy, but they are important as emergency reserves and a parking place for future investments.

- *Real estate* involves land and/or buildings. These investments are usually quite costly and not very liquid.

- *Commodities* are tangible goods such as grains, metals, and foods. Investing in commodities is normally too complicated and risky for the average investor.

The entire world of investments fits neatly into these five categories. To paraphrase economist John Kenneth Galbraith, there is nothing about these five categories that can't be understood by any person with reasonable curiosity. And even then, generally speaking, most of us, for investment purposes, will only be involved in the first three—stocks, bonds, and cash. (We'll be discussing these three categories in later chapters.)

Sounds simple enough. And it is. Investing is essentially a simple process with complex variations. You don't have to be a genius in math or have a master's degree in business to learn it. You don't need a trust fund or a tremendous salary. You *do* need the desire to learn and the fortitude to buck traditions that no longer apply. Armed with these qualities, you'll be amazed at what can follow.

Money magazine conducted a study to find out what happens when women become familiar with finances. In a June 1992 article, big bold letters heralded the answer: "WOMEN ARE OFTEN SMARTER THAN MEN ABOUT MONEY." They proved themselves, said the text, "not only as capable as men but superior to them in several ways."

According to this study, women ask more questions, do their homework, seek help more often, set goals, and take more conservative risks.

(Men, on the other hand, tend to think they know more than they do, ask fewer questions and request help less often, act on hot tips rather than solid research, and take more hazardous risks.)

I frequently asked financial professionals if they noticed a difference between the sexes. Their answers were markedly similar. "I can count maybe thirty seconds before a woman starts telling me how stupid she is," stockbroker Esther Berger observed. "These women are the brightest I've known; they clearly didn't get where they are by magic. But they feel incredibly stupid." Not men, though. "I've never had a man walk into my office and tell me he's stupid," she noted. "He usually assumes he knows more than I do. That's a fundamental difference I see. Men usually assume they know more than they do. Women assume they are stupid and border-line uneducable."

Experts agree, however, that once educated, *women indisputably have what it takes to become damn good investors.* In fact, according to the National Association of Investors Corporation, women's investment clubs regularly outperform men's investment clubs in average annual return.

Getting smart with money has nothing to do with genes or gender, just as it has no relation to genius. It has everything to do with the learning curve. Lacking this awareness, we're likely to get frustrated and give up when it seems we're getting nowhere. That's exactly what happened to me. I'd try to learn about money but always quit in frustration when I couldn't see progress. All that changed when I understood the way the learning curve works.

An Out-of-Body Experience

I remember the exact moment I got it. I had just come home from yet another class about money management. But on this particular evening, something astounding occurred. I had an inexplicable urge to sit down and read my trust statement. I couldn't believe it! This document was about as appealing (and coherent) to me as a calculus text would be to a toddler. Sometimes, when I met with financial professionals, I brought my statement along. "This is a very conservative portfolio," they would say. I had no idea what that meant. They would patiently explain everything, but their words, like rising steam from a boiling kettle, floated right over my head.

On this particular night, however, I picked up the most recent statement from a pile on my desk and actually read it—and the strangest thing happened. Every word, every number, on that document was completely clear! I read through the whole thing line by line and never spaced out. The fog had lifted. I could see that my money was invested in real estate, municipal bonds, treasury bills, and cash. No stocks. So that's what they meant by conservative, I mused. No stocks.

Then, to my utter astonishment, I figured out which bonds paid the lowest yields and concluded I'd sell those to settle my tax bill. It was as if I were standing outside myself, absolutely flabbergasted at what I saw: a woman who looked just like me, reading about investments like a pro. "How did that happen?" I wondered incredulously.

Of course, there was nothing mysterious about this sudden comprehension. It was the outcome of all the work I had been doing: taking classes, reading books, asking questions, all my sporadic, halfhearted attempts to understand finances. What made it different this time was that I hadn't given up. Propelled by the inspiring women I was interviewing, I kept plugging away. This was not some lucky fluke. I had finally come to the tail end of a very long learning curve.

In a way, the learning curve does resemble magic. Results that appear impossibly out of reach one day can be unexpectedly manifest the next. But once we understand how this happens, we realize there is nothing mystical about it. Learning follows a logical and predictable process. Results don't show up immediately; they develop like a Polaroid picture. Clarity is the outcome of a process that takes time. And I'm convinced that the process is made easier with understanding.

It's a process that occurs automatically, naturally, anytime we learn something new or add to what we know. But we are usually unconscious, unaware of its presence. If we could shift our perspective just slightly, if we could look at the experience of taking control of our money as a heroic journey rather than a hopeless predicament, then maybe what feels menacing could become meaningful. Instead of regarding confusion, fear, and discomfort as signs that something is wrong, we could take them as an indication that something is changing.

Charting the Learning Curve

If we were to draw a map of the learning process, it would resemble a U-shaped curve. Along this U-shaped curve lie four sequential psychological stages. In order to complete the learning curve, we must pass through each of these four stages. They are:

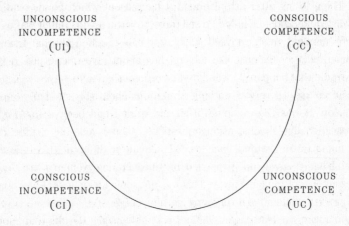

UNCONSCIOUS
INCOMPETENCE
(UI)

CONSCIOUS
COMPETENCE
(CC)

CONSCIOUS
INCOMPETENCE
(CI)

UNCONSCIOUS
COMPETENCE
(UC)

- *Unconscious Incompetence*
- *Conscious Incompetence*
- *Unconscious Competence*
- *Conscious Competence.*

Let's look at what we can expect as we encounter each of the four stages.

1. Unconscious Incompetence

There is a story about the great Paderewski, who was approached by a woman after one of his concerts. "Oh, maestro," she cried, "you are such a genius."

"But, madame," the pianist protested, "before I was a genius, I was nothing."

That is how the learning curve begins—knowing nothing. In this first stage, *Unconscious Incompetence,* we don't even know what we don't know. We are literally in the dark. I spent most of my adult life in the first stage. I had no idea how much money I had, where it was, or what my husband was doing with it. And truth be told, I didn't care. Whoever coined the phrase "Ignorance is bliss" was no doubt referring to the first stage of the learning curve. There is a tremendous temptation to stay put at this stage. But the ATM's refusing to give me money was the kick I needed to start the learning curve. Remember, however, we don't need to wait for a crisis to begin the process. In fact, by understanding how the learning curve works, we can save ourselves a lot of anguish and lost time by choosing to jump aboard.

I remember Carla—a slender, plain-faced young woman, dressed in frayed jeans, who grew up on a cotton farm in the Deep South—as a stunning example of someone who avoided calamity by being proactive. Carla was an artist with meager earnings and a tiny inheritance (from the sale of the family farm when her parents died), who had become alarmed by her shrinking bank balance. We sat in her small kitchen, surrounded by children's art tacked on the walls—souvenirs from classes she had taught, she proudly explained, then she recounted her early experiences trying to get a grip on her money. "In the beginning I knew nothing, nothing at all. I just knew I had to learn," she told me, wincing at the uncomfortable recollection. "This was not the way I wanted to spend my time. I was an artist, a free spirit, a free spender. But I knew it was my future at stake. I was spending principal. If I didn't do something soon, I'd have nothing left. I knew I had to throw myself into learning this stuff wholeheartedly." The first thing she did was take a class in basic finance.

2. Conscious Incompetence

We enter the second stage of the learning curve—*Conscious Incompetence*—the moment we take our first steps toward learning: when we attend our first finance class, glance at the stock reports, or leaf through *Money* magazine. This stage can be a disturbing experience. Whereas up to now we didn't recognize the extent of our ignorance, suddenly we're stuck by how uninformed we actually are. And the more we learn, it seems, the more baffled we become. This can be an utterly discouraging, totally bewildering period. The subject seems immense, and mastery feels unattainable.

If the previous stage, blissful ignorance, is one people don't want to leave, Conscious Incompetence is the stage most people can't wait to flee. Here it takes unswerving commitment to keep going.

When I asked Carla how she felt once she got started, she replied: "I was scared to death. My first thought was, Oh, my God, I want someone else to do this. It felt like such a huge responsibility. I didn't know anything."

Carla wasn't sure why she was so scared. After all, she was a college graduate, she wasn't dumb, she knew she was capable of learning. But there she was, sitting in a class, scared to death. Carla, of course, didn't realize she was describing the second stage of the learning curve. As she explained, "I just stayed in the moment, paced myself, and did what I could do."

These first two stages don't feel great, but they have a purpose. Whether we're "phenomenally unknowledgeable," as a friend once described herself, or we've come so far but still have a way to go, not-knowing is actually a good place to start. It is the Zen mind, the empty mind ready to be filled. If we think we know everything, it's harder to learn.

3. Unconscious Competence

By the time we reach the third stage of the learning curve—*Unconscious Competence*—we've begun to absorb what we've been studying. Still, we're wondering if anything has sunk in. In this stage we don't realize how much we actually know. We've spent time reading, practicing, studying, researching, but we're essentially unaware of any progress. Occasionally, we get glimpses, but the fog has yet to lift completely. During this stage, we may have spurts of improvement, flashes of understanding. Someone will mention an investment concept, and it makes perfect sense. But these moments are fleeting, mere hints of what's around the corner.

"Somewhere along the way," Carla noted, "it got easier, and I started thinking maybe this money stuff is doable. But it took a while before I was convinced." She likened the experience to starting art school, wondering if she had enough talent to succeed, but feeling more confident after a few courses. Carla was clearly at stage three. At this point, we have no idea how far along we really are. Gradually, if we just hang in there long enough, we'll enter the last stage, where everything comes together.

4. Conscious Competence

In this last stage, *Conscious Competence,* we finally realize how competent we've become. After weeks, maybe months, of frustration, we see the light, and we actually feel smarter, speak intelligently, make prudent decisions. This awareness may come suddenly, as it did for me when I analyzed my trust statement and made informed decisions on future investments, or it may emerge gradually. There's still more to learn, but we now have an indisputable grasp of the subject. Information begins to make sense. We start to feel in control.

I remember Carla grinning proudly when she told me about a meeting she once had with a stockbroker. "Toward the end [of the learning process], I was talking to this broker and he thought I worked in the field." She beamed. "It's been very empowering."

We traverse these four stages every time we acquire new skills. Our pace may vary, but the process won't. We may zip through all four stages, get bogged down in one, or move back and forth between several. It's different each time. Carla told me it took her seven months to feel comfortably knowledgeable. Some women progress faster, others much more slowly. Our speed depends in large part on our degree of motivation, our prior education, and the amount of time we allot to studying. Normally, there is rapid growth in the early stages; the later stages go slower. There is a reason for this slowdown.

Warning: Overwhelm Happens

Somewhere between *Conscious Incompetence* and *Conscious Competence*, when all we can see is how little we know and how much more there is to learn, we run smack-dab into *overwhelm*—that omigod-I'll-never-understand-all-this-stuff feeling. For a fortunate few, the feelings of overwhelm are momentary, hardly noticeable; they're barely bothered by it. "There is a part of me that doesn't understand why learning about money is such an issue for people," one woman remarked. "For me, it's just another detail of life."

For most of us, however, overwhelm is impossible to ignore. Overwhelm is a sensation of utter confusion that feels as if it will last forever. We know we're in overwhelm when we catch ourselves saying things like: "I am so confused"; "Nothing makes sense"; "I feel stuck." This period is marked by uncertainty, anxiety, even hopelessness and apathy. We become filled with self-doubt. We bounce from emotion to emotion—anger, fear, frustration, even depression.

Carla, for example, told me she sat through an entire finance class, listening to the teacher and wondering, What the heck does all this mean?

"I felt totally in the dark," she recalled. "I could not get the language. It was all way too abstract. I felt I'd never understand this stuff."

Many of us don't realize that feelings of overwhelm come with the territory. Overwhelm is an inevitable part of our initiation into the ranks of the financially enlightened. But gratefully, overwhelm is only temporary, usually short-lived, and it invariably passes. However, since this is not a topic generally discussed in financial literature, overwhelm is often mistaken for terminal stupidity.

I remember a conversation I had with a new acquaintance. She was a CPA, a chief financial officer at a bank, and had majored in finance, yet she'd never invested in the market and was struggling to get started. "It's taking me such a long time," she moaned. "There is this inertia, like I'm in a holding pattern. I get really mad I'm so lazy. But I'm so confused about what to do."

This woman was neither lazy nor stupid. She was in overwhelm. But instead of seeing overwhelm as a normal phase in the process of learning, she felt like a failure. This is what happens: Our lack of progress produces a loss of confidence. We're convinced this is our fate forever. We want to give up.

What most of us fail to appreciate during these periods of confusion and inertia is that tremendous progress is actually occurring. Though we don't know it, can't see it, it's like a garden in winter—there is life stirring beneath the surface. The information we're absorbing is being assimilated. This is not a stagnant state. It is a fallow time, a necessary phase in the natural cycle of growth.

George Leonard, in his insightful book *Mastery*, refers to this phase as "the Plateau." Learning takes place when you're on the Plateau, not in the spurt upward," he writes. But "to the goal-oriented person, the Plateau can be purgatory."

Overwhelm may feel like hell, but this period has a purpose. It's meant to be a moratorium. Financial planner Ashland O'Coyle calls this phenomenon "the Pause." "The Pause is when you become overwhelmed and you stop," she explains. "Most people interpret it as paralysis. It's not. It's a healthy part of the process. It's just a pause where the rest of your emotions catch up to the place where you are."

It gives us time to catch our breath, recharge our batteries, digest what we've learned. It prevents us from taking imprudent actions, making impetuous choices, or pursuing goals before we have the capacity to achieve them. "I see my paralysis has kept me from being impulsive," one woman told me. "It has forced me to go slow, use restraint, and make good decisions."

In the creative process, this phase is known as an incubation period. In the hero's journey, it's the time in the wilderness. "Most heroic journeys involve going through a dark place," mythologist Jean Shinoda Bolen once explained, "through mountain caverns, the underworld, or labyrinth passages, to emerge finally into the light."

Psychologically, we are leaving a condition of ignorance and childlike dependency to become informed adults taking responsibility for our lives.

Overwhelm marks the time between, the gap between what was and what will be. This is where our old assumptions start to disintegrate, outdated beliefs collide with new expectations. "It's an empty space," writes William Bridges, author of *Transitions*, "within which a new sense of self can gestate." Change, any change, will throw a system into chaos. Overwhelm is an empty space where chaos thrives.

Chaos is not just senseless turmoil. It is the birthplace for all beginnings, the darkness from which all creation emanates. When chaos is allowed to run its course, order naturally evolves out of chaos.

"Look for integration," says psychologist Ira Progoff in *The Practice of Process Meditation*, "in the depths of the darkest moment, where the confusion and disorganization is at its fullest. There is where it is beginning to form itself."

Unfortunately, this is exactly where most of us want to call it quits. The problem is not overwhelm. The problem is our negative reaction to feeling overwhelmed. We detest uncertainty. We find the chaos and confusion intolerable. We try to impose our own order, to control that which feels uncontrollable, to make sense of things that don't make sense. Either we strive harder, keep floundering, feel stupid, and stop trying, or we go back to the way we've always done things. Not surprisingly, we create the same outcomes as before.

There is another way to get through this period, a far more productive way. This approach calls for persistence, patience, and consistency. We need to keep doing whatever we can do, at the pace we can do it. We need to keep educating ourselves to the best of our ability, even if nothing makes sense. When I asked women I interviewed what they did while they were in the throes of overwhelm, they all said pretty much the same thing. They hung in there. They kept doing the footwork despite their frustrations. "I kept plugging away," is what I heard so often. Or, as Carla told me, "I just stayed in the moment, paced myself, and did what I could do."

Eventually overwhelm dissipates. Confusion will give way to comprehension. It probably won't happen overnight, though it could. More likely, the confusion will subside gradually, though not necessarily smoothly. Natural evolution proceeds in fits and starts. So it is with our financial evolution.

One woman put it like this: "When I first started making good money, I was intimidated by the decisions I had to make. For a long time, all I felt was overwhelm and paralysis." What did she do? "I took a lot of work-shops, and I did a lot of studying," she explained. "It's been hit or miss. But I'm making decisions now, and it feels awfully good to be out of paralysis."

Riding the Learning Curve

Using a real-life example, let's see what this journey along the learning curve actually looks like. We met Renee in Chapter Three. She told us she had spent her life waiting for Prince Charming, but a messy divorce had shattered the myth, leaving her feeling, like her maiden aunt, that some-thing was "intrinsically wrong" with her. She had no background in finance, nor, at the time, did she have much money. But once she realized her white knight wasn't coming, she knew it was time to start learning.

"How did you start?" I asked. "What was the first thing you did?"

"I started going to free seminars," Renee told me. "I didn't have enough money to invest, but it didn't matter. I was on a discovery mission. I was just finding out information. What I started realizing was how much I didn't know. They'd use terms and I had no idea what they meant. I'd get lost in the jargon, so I'd ask a lot of questions. I'd say, Could you explain that a little more thoroughly? Then I would get more information." *(Renee is leaving stage one: Unconscious Incompetence, and entering stage two: Conscious Incompetence.)*

Something very interesting happens when we make the transition from stage one to stage two—fate often intervenes. Once we commit to the learning process, we are frequently assisted by a phenomenon known as synchronicity. Call it *"the luck of the learning curve."* Fortuitous coinci-dences and unforeseen opportunities appear out of nowhere, almost as if invisible guides were directing our way. We flip through a magazine article and get an idea for something else. One thing leads to another. In Renee's case, she found a new job that changed everything.

While still going to seminars, Renee was hired to do marketing for an investment company. One day, her boss walked in and told her he needed a comparison of three different investments. He dropped them on her desk and walked out. "I had no idea what to do," she recalls. "How do you compare an investment? I had no clue."

So she went to the firm's attorney. "How do you compare investments?" she asked him.

"Read the prospectus," he said.

"What's a prospectus?" she asked.

He took the material her boss had given her, pulled out the prospectuses, and handed them to her.

"What am I supposed to read?" she asked.

"Everything," he answered.

She went back to her desk, sat down with a highlighter in one hand, the documents in the other, a pad of paper in front of her, and began. *(The ubiquitous overwhelm is about to appear.)*

"I felt totally overwhelmed. I didn't understand more than two lines before I had to stop and read it again. It took me days to go through them. I'd have to get up, walk around, come back, read it again, get up, walk around, come back," she said.

"I'd go through the documents, underline what I understood, then I'd look at it. If it was something I thought I wanted to remember, I wrote it down."

Meanwhile, she kept going to free seminars. She also started reading: *Forbes*, the *Wall Street Journal*, *Money* magazine. She didn't read everything in the publications, she explained, just the articles that interested her. *(She zips to stage three: Unconscious Competence.)*

"After a while it got so that I could jump through prospectuses fairly easily. They started making more and more sense to me. The haze began to disappear, and I understood more and more of what was going on. From reading and doing what I did, I lost my fear of prospectuses. It's one thing I learned—no matter what, just keep at it. I kept plugging away. I ended up being the expert in the company. I found things in prospectuses that no one else found." *(Finally, stage four: Conscious Competence.)*

Rules of the Road

Traveling the learning curve is not complicated, but it is challenging. Psychologists tell us that change is always met with resistance. Without fail, the moment we step on this path of learning, resistance, like a growling dog guarding the gate, is there to block our way—warning us to stay away. We don't feel right. We get scared. We want to quit. At the same time, something internal urges us forward. Staying with the learning curve is not easy, especially when we're awash with feelings of over-whelm. But I have discovered that if we just start, keep going, and never give up, Conscious Competence is guaranteed.

Getting Started

"I remember being determined to play tennis," financial talk show host Terry Savage told me. "I went every Saturday and I learned. It's a skill, just like money. You don't have to have a special talent. You don't have to be a genius. You just need to start."

Good advice, and easy to follow. There's one catch, though—we must be motivated to start. We need an incentive. There are two kinds of heroes, Joseph Campbell once said. "Some that *chose* to undertake the journey. And some that didn't." When I asked women what moved them onto the learning curve, their answers fell into these two categories. There were those catapulted onto the learning curve by some kind of crisis. Others, like Carla, were smarter. These women initiated the process voluntarily, motivated by some internal drive, either curiosity or concern, eagerness or anxiety.

"This is not something I was interested in," Carla said, sighing, "but I developed food allergies and I wasn't interested in diet or nutrition either. I had to learn in order to figure out what I was going to do. It's just some-thing you force your brain to do. That's the same thing I did with money."

These were the women I wanted to learn from. "How did you get started?" I would ask them during our interviews.

"I signed up for a series of financial planning seminars," said Carla, who realized that as an artist, she had severely neglected the more rational and practical side of life. As a result of the seminars, she explained, "I got in the habit of writing down everything I spent. It forced me to be aware. It helped me become responsible."

"All I did was read and ask people questions. I'd ask people what books they liked, and I'd read them," another woman answered. "People would say to me, 'Have you thought about XYZ?' Then I'd ask someone else what they knew about XYZ. I did this for three or four months. Just by asking questions and reading, I found out I could do this. I didn't feel helpless like before."

"At first all I did was subscribe to the *Wall Street Journal*," another told me. "Every time I opened it, I felt I was exposing myself to financial issues. I think, by osmosis, I picked up some investment knowledge. I also joined an investment club. I considered the $20 monthly fee my tuition. It was a fabulous education."

"I went to the library and got books on the market," one business-woman said. "I figured money is a science, like biology, and there were certain things I had to know. I also subscribed to the *Wall Street Journal*, *Fortune*, *Money* magazine, anything I thought would help me. Sure enough, the more I read, the more I understood."

"I took the teacher's approach," a former teacher explained. "I talked to people. I kept asking questions and took notes on everything they told me."

Over and over I heard what these women did. It became a no-brainer. I started doing the same things. I subscribed to the *Wall Street Journal* and other publications. Some I read, others I scanned quickly. I wrote away for every free publication I saw on the subject—there was a surprising number of great freebies. I listened to audiocassettes about financial topics, such as Peter Lynch's books on tape. I'd meet with friends and ask what they were doing with their money. I joined the American Association of Individual Investors. I started attending workshops and lectures—some were free, some weren't. I formed an investment club with a group of friends, and we met monthly. I asked to pick the brain of every financial expert I came across. I did whatever I could do. And for a long time, I felt I was groping blindly in the dark, getting absolutely nowhere.

Perseverance Pays Off

"The thing I learned was just to do one step at a time," Carla told me. "That's been very useful to me. It's not so much that I should have the financial manager now or I should have settled with the bank or whatever. The thing to do right now is write this letter or make this phone call or read this book or talk to this person. Quite often what happens is I make the phone call and then there is something else I've got to do."

That's exactly how we proceed through the learning curve. One step at a time. Learning occurs in small increments, through daily efforts, with gradual progress. "Whoever wants to reach a distant goal," observed the German scholar Helmut Schmidt, "must take many small steps."

When you come right down to it, successful learning is determined by one factor and one factor only: commitment. Once we commit ourselves, the odds are stacked in our favor. Commitment is what keeps us from quitting when we meet with disappointment, feel overpowered by overwhelm, or fall flat on our face.

When I think of commitment, I am reminded of a story about a snail climbing a cherry tree during a blizzard. A squirrel peeks out and sees the snail inching its way along the trunk.

"Where are you going?" the squirrel asks.

"To get some cherries," the snail answers.

"It's the middle of winter!" cries the squirrel. "There aren't any cherries up there."

The snail, never stopping, glances over at the squirrel and replies, "There will be by the time I get there."

This is the kind of tenacity and unbending intent we need to develop. We need to be firmly committed to our goal—financial responsibility—even if the outcome seems impossibly out of reach. The stronger our motivation and desire, the more likely we are to stick with it. What we discover, in time, is that the pursuit of knowledge itself spontaneously generates action. Noted physician and author Deepak Chopra writes about this phenomenon in his best-selling book *Creating Affluence*. "Organizing power is inherent in knowledge," he says. "Knowledge of any kind gets metabolized spontaneously and brings about a change in awareness from where it is possible to create new realities."

Gaining knowledge, Chopra declares, is far more potent than excessive effort. Simply by becoming knowledgeable in a certain area, such as money, we automatically create conditions for achieving proficiency. Invariably, the more we study a certain subject—any subject—the easier it becomes to do and the less resistance we have to tackling it.

Tools for the Traveler

When traveling the learning curve, I have found five activities that are particularly helpful. These five courses of action, like a reassuring hand against our back, will fortify our efforts, expedite our progress, and enhance our eventual success. They are:

1. Seek support
2. Find a mentor
3. Learn by doing
4. Get organized
5. Feel the feelings

1. Seek support

We don't have to travel this path alone. As we start on our way, it's important to solicit support. We can join an investment club, form a support group, or talk to friends. "My advice," says Linda Pei, of the Women's Equity Mutual Fund, "is to take a friend and do it together. You don't have to be alone in this. Everybody feels the same way. So go find another person just like you. Learn together." Carla, as we'll see later, joined a twelve-step support group, Debtors Anonymous.

2. Find a mentor

Many of the women I interviewed had support not just from a group or a fellow seeker but from a knowledgeable mentor. A husband, friend, a financial professional, helped them learn by pushing them to participate and personally tutoring them.

Pamela, a former schoolteacher, now an entrepreneur, did quite well investing in real estate. She credits her boyfriend, Alex, with teaching her everything she knows. I was particularly intrigued by a comment she made during our interview: "One of my girlfriends, maybe ten years ago, when Alex was a builder, said to him, 'Why don't you give Pamela one of those units?' He answered, 'No, the best gift I could ever give Pamela is to teach her how to buy it for herself.'"

Stories like Pamela's pushed me to find a mentor too. I was at the point (somewhere in the Unconscious Competence stage) where I knew in theory what to do, but I was reluctant to dive in. However, when the student is ready, so the saying goes, the teacher appears. His name was Peter Camejo, a stockbroker who specializes in socially responsible investments. He lectured at a class I was attending. He spoke so enthusiastically and passionately about how a person's investment could make a difference in the world that I called him for an appointment.

I met him at his office and gave him a brief rundown of my struggle with money. He listened carefully. "This is what I propose," he said after I finished. "You give me a sum of money—nothing you can't afford to lose. Our purpose will not be to make money. It will be to teach you about your investments. Then you can decide what you want to do."

Over the next six months, we bought preferred stocks, convertible bonds, closed-end funds. We placed stop-loss orders and drew up a profit and loss statement. We even invested in risky options, like puts and calls, my ex-husband's undoing, because, as Peter explained, "You'll decide whether or not to trade in options because you understand them, not because your husband lost money on them." (I decided they weren't for me.) We went over every statement, every transaction slip, until he was sure I understood everything.

When I started, I didn't know what half the terms meant, despite all the reading and studying I had done. A convertible bond? A closed-end fund? A stop-loss order? But after a few months, there wasn't an expert around with whom I couldn't carry on a lucid conversation. I am a firm believer that we learn best by doing. Which brings us to the third technique.

3. Learn by doing

Reading, talking to people, attending classes, are important steps. But book knowledge is not enough. If we want to understand investing, putting even a little bit of money into the market—no more than we can afford to lose—will teach us far more than standing on the sidelines. "Though you can read many books about investments, you can never learn unless you become a player," wrote Bennett Goodspeed in his classic *The Tao Jones Averages*. "[Investing] can be known only through doing, as that is how you can best acquire a feel."

If we're going to learn how to invest, we must actually do it. Trial and error is essential to the learning curve. I began to notice that a lot of women I interviewed dabbled in the market in order to learn. Remember Gayle, who walked out of Charles Schwab in a daze? She didn't give up. When she called me, so distraught, I suggested she join the investment club I had started. After our club made its first investment—in Merck, a drug company—Gayle went out and invested some of her own money in it as well.

"I listened to people explain their research and concluded Merck would be a smart buy," she explained to me. "Well, Merck actually went down after the group bought it. So I reasoned that if it was a good buy at $35, maybe it was an even better buy at $29. Having nothing better to guide me, I got 100 shares. In the next eight or nine months, it bounced gradually up to $42. That sucker is worth over $4,000 today."

Of course, not all investments will go up. But her experience taught Gayle, more than any book or article could have, how investing works. Not long ago, Gayle called me. "I am somebody who reads the *Wall Street Journal* every day and I feel like a very different woman." She laughed excitedly. "You can ask me whether the market is up or the dollar is weak, and I'd actually know the answer! It is the start of a new mind-set about money, and a whole new self-image."

4. Get organized

One thing's for sure—from the moment we invest, we'll be besieged with paperwork. The sooner we start organizing this information, the saner we'll stay. Most women I interviewed developed some sort of system, whether it was using file folders or three-ring binders, for keeping their statements, transaction slips, and any relevant material in some kind of order. Following their examples, I set up one notebook for my mutual funds and another for my stocks. I keep articles in file folders. This has made my financial life infinitely easier to stay on top of.

"When I started, I was totally disorganized," Carla told me. "I couldn't keep up with the unbelievable amount of mail that comes every day." Her solution was to attend an organizational workshop. "They told me to store everything in files. If I put it in piles, I'm lost. Now I have files for everything—projects, accounts, people. I save everything relevant, and I try not to handle a piece of paper too many times."

Another woman admitted, "If you asked me to name all my stocks, I couldn't do it. But if I go upstairs to my file, I could pull out the list of every one I own. I have all the statements filed and organized."

Organization minimizes overwhelm—though it probably won't eliminate it.

5. Feel the feelings

When we run into overwhelm, as surely we will, we can respond in one of two ways: We can repress our feelings, lapse into old habits, and never progress. Or we can experience those feelings, without fighting or judging them. If we can stay with the overwhelm, riding confusion like a surfer riding the waves, we will be carried beyond the familiar to unforeseen possibilities.

"It was really an unsettling time." Carla remembered how she felt during her first finance class. "It was very painful at first. Everyone else seemed to understand what was going on. I was so confused I didn't even know what questions to ask. But I hung in there. I knew it was something I needed to do."

The key is not to resist the confusion, discomfort, and frustration, but to allow these feelings to run their course. Recognize this as part of the journey, a private rite of passage. It is a time to surrender, feel our feelings, let overwhelm exist, but remain on the learning curve. Surrender does not imply passivity in the context of the curve; it signifies acceptance of what is and an unyielding desire for what can be.

Though no end may be in sight, proceed as if there will be one. If we just keep going and don't give up, changes will occur. Trust that the chaos will eventually rearrange itself into a new order.

I once read a beautiful description of the benefits of patient persistence. "When nothing seems to help, I go and look at a stonecutter hammering away at his rocks, perhaps a hundred times without as much as a crack showing in it. Yet at the 101st blow it will split in two, and I know it was not that blow that did it, but all that had gone before."

What Happens When Resistance Takes Over?

Abraham Maslow, a father of modern psychological thinking, wrote that all learning is determined by the relationship of two forces within us. One is fear, which keeps us clinging to safety, and the other is desire, which drives us forward to the full functioning of our capability. "We grow forward," he observed, "when the delights of growth and anxieties of safety are greater than the anxieties of growth and the delights of safety."

Such was the case for many of the smart women I interviewed. They stuck with the learning curve, pushing through overwhelm like a snail in a snowstorm, and their stories have a happy ending. But what happens when anxiety far outweighs the delights? We read, study, research, do all the things we're supposed to, yet instead of advancing, we seem to be anchored. Just one step at a time, we're told. But we can't even figure out what that next step is. Nor is emotional surrender, dogged persistence, or even peer support enough to get us going. Sometimes, resistance takes over and undermines our every success. It can keep us feeling stupid and stagnant. It virtually paralyzes many of us. Is this common? Yes! Is there hope? Yes! To get out from under, however, we may need to turn inward. That is the message that awaits us in the next realization.

··· **CHAPTER FOUR RECAPPED** ···

Realization: There is a learning curve to financial proficiency. The learning curve is a process with four sequential stages that takes us from unconscious incompetence to conscious competence. Completing this process requires that we deal as much with feelings as with facts and relies as much on tenacity and courage as on reading books and taking classes.

To Do

1. Make a list of educational activities you can do. Your computer, the local newspaper, any financial publication, is a gold mine of resources. Keep an eye out for seminars, lectures, brochures, and financial materials. Take advantage of the free classes and workbooks most investment firms offer—some of them are quite good—but be wary of high-pressured sales tactics.

2. Set up a schedule for financial education: sign up for a class, buy a book, talk to a certain person, log on the Internet. Assign a specific time for each activity by writing it in your calendar, just as you do your other time commitments.

3. Do something every day, even if it's just glancing at the *Wall Street Journal* on your way to work. You could listen to the nightly business report while cooking dinner, flip through a copy of *Smart Money* magazine at the newsstand, drop by the library and check out a book by Peter Lynch (his books are truly delightful, enjoyable reading) or pick up *Personal Finance for Dummies*, by Eric Tyson, a very easy read.

4. Find a buddy, someone who will do this right along with you and hold you accountable. Check in with each other on a regular basis to report your progress, exchange moral support, reward your efforts, celebrate your successes.

5. To minimize overwhelm, start organizing financial materials immediately. Buy a pile of file folders or some three-ring binders. Every time you make notes during a class, receive a relevant brochure, clip an informative article, or simply get an idea, drop it in the appropriately labeled file or staple it onto a page in the appropriate section of a notebook. The sooner you begin, the easier it is.

Chapter Five

• •

Realization #3
All the Answers Aren't Out There

> *He who knows much about others may be learned*
> *but he who understands himself is more intelligent.*
> *He who controls others may be powerful, but he*
> *who masters himself, is mightier still.*
>
> —*Lao-tzu*

It is the first day of a course titled "Women, Money, and Power." The students, of whom I am one, are seated in a circle. In the middle of the circle is a curious sight—a clump of white netting like a bridal veil, flung carelessly to the floor. Without preamble, the instructor walks over to the netting, scoops it up, and, looking around the circle, announces, "This is what we're going to do in this class. We are going to lift the veils that cloud our understanding of money." Underneath the white netting lies the *Wall Street Journal*.

"To lift the veils," the instructor continues, "we have to get in touch with the decisions we've made about money, most of which were made early in life and are now unconscious. These decisions are like veils that get in the way of our financial understanding.

"The more we can see in here," the instructor continues, patting her head, "the more we can see out there." She points to the *Journal*.

I was impressed. This was the first finance class I had attended that not only addressed the usual topics, such as budgets, credit, investments, and insurance, but also had us explore our attitudes, beliefs, and mind-sets around money. I discovered later what had prompted the instructor to include the psychological component: her personal experience. At the time she taught this class, Abby was the director of the MBA program at a local university. She had a degree in economics, an extensive background in banking and financial services, and a history of neglect in managing her own money.

"I had all the technical information to act in a responsible way," she confessed during our interview, "but I wasn't doing it. I'd ignore my finances or deal with them halfheartedly. I was very ashamed of this. I knew what to do, I was doing it for others, but not for me. I was trustee of my dad's estate. I kept wonderful records for him. But when it came to my personal records, forget it."

Eventually Abby came to a crucial understanding. "I realized I had some deeper issues," she said. "It was as if I felt I wasn't important or worthy enough. I knew I'd better start working on what was going on underneath my irresponsibility."

Often, probably more than most of us realize, our financial problems have nothing to do with money per se. So many times, regardless of our IQ, education, or experience, we find ourselves behaving in disturbingly irresponsible ways—by overspending, excessive thrift, or, in Abby's case, sheer negligence. We start the learning curve but get stuck or sidetracked. These behaviors can show up early, when we're just getting started, or later, after we've made considerable progress. We know what to do; we just don't do it. These behaviors are not the problem. They are merely symptoms of something deeper. Therefore, we're not going to find solutions to those problems "out there"—in another finance book, with a new advisor, or from some other source of external knowledge. We need to look beyond the intellect. That doesn't mean we should ignore the technical information. But as Abby explained to me, "The practical and psychological have to be interwoven. I had to keep going between the two."

The same may hold true for many of us. While we are learning the facts and figures, we may also need to examine our blocks and barriers. Psychological insight can be every bit as important as practical information in the reaching of our financial goals. For some of us, this realization that *all the answers aren't out there* could be the most critical realization of all.

I have a friend who is very knowledgeable about finances and quite a go-getter in business. Recently, she complained that despite her best intentions, she's been ignoring her investments and she's baffled by her passivity.

"I know I should do something," she groaned, "but it's like taking medicine. I keep saying to myself, 'I know it's good for me! I know it's good for me!'"

But knowing what to do and doing it are two different things. It's like losing weight. We all know how to do it—eat less and exercise more. Managing money is just as straightforward—spend less, save more, and invest well. But when, try as we may, we can't shed the pounds or get a grip on our finances, odds are we need to look deeper. Perhaps unconscious motives oppose our conscious intentions.

"We can go and sit in on class after class and find the best investment advisor," financial psychologist Kathleen Gurney told me. "But it's acting on that advice and education that makes the difference. Often what prevents us from acting are those unconscious feelings and attitudes that are driving our behavior."

A Snag in the Learning Curve

That certainly was the case for me. Here I was, sailing along, finally understanding what I was reading, considering myself on top of this "money stuff," when suddenly I found myself besieged by resistance. I put off doing anything financially related. I'd toss out the *Wall Street Journal* without reading it. I'd make a list of advisors to call and forget to make the calls. And I'd watch myself "going stupid" when I talked to friends about money. I was acutely aware of what I was doing but completely unable to change.

After months of frustration, I went to see a psychologist. As soon as I sat down, my frustration poured out. "I want to be smart with money,"

I cried. "I really want to be good with this stuff, but I keep procrastinating. I feel like I'm never going to take charge." I babbled on and on about how stuck I felt and how frustrated I was, when Daniel interrupted me.

"Let's try something," he said. He moved into another chair. "I'll be a voice in your head, your voice. You go on telling me about how badly you want to learn about money, and I'll respond as your voice. Then I want you to dialogue with this voice."

"Okay," I said, and I proceeded to rant about how much I wanted to be smart with money.

Daniel, speaking as my alter ego, interrupted me. "No you don't," he challenged. "You don't really want to know about money. You talk about it a lot, but you don't really want to be smart."

I tried to disagree, but I couldn't. I didn't have the energy to argue. That voice he spoke in was indeed inside me, and it was stronger than I had ever imagined. In that instant, I realized there was a part of me, a huge part, that did not want to be financially responsible. For years I had been trying to repress this voice. I had been afraid that if I let it speak, it would take over. In truth, my repression gave it power. That part of me *had* taken over.

Over the next several weeks, with Daniel's help, I got to know that part of me. I let that part talk, heard what it had to say, what it was afraid of, and what its payoff was for staying ignorant. I learned how very scared I was of making mistakes and losing everything. I saw how nervous I was over my family's reaction if I changed. I realized that despite my progress, I still saw myself as stupid. But what surprised me most were my fears of being abandoned. What I thought had ended with my divorce—the belief that I had to be weak to be loved—still clung tenaciously to my brain, like barnacles to a ship.

"No wonder you're afraid to get smart," Daniel said gently. "Staying stupid has become an act of self-preservation."

This awareness alone parted the veils for me. Once I recognized what was blocking my way, I had little trouble getting past it. Trying to overcome resistance through sheer determination can be a monumental, if not impossible, task. But once we discover what internal barriers impede our progress, lifting the veils can happen spontaneously, almost effortlessly.

The Veil of Fears

> *"Money ranks with love as man's greatest source of joy and with death as his greatest source of anxiety."*
>
> —JOHN KENNETH GALBRAITH

Wait a minute! you're probably saying to yourself. What's all this talk about shrinks and self-exploration? Isn't this a book about money? Why do we need to delve into our psyches?

For one simple reason. Like it or not, our state of mind directly affects our course of action—the way we earn, spend, and invest our money. We can never completely separate our private emotions from our personal finances. "Money is a far more emotional topic than most people acknowledge," writes Phil Laut in his splendid book, *Money Is My Friend*. Abby agrees wholeheartedly. "Almost all the decisions we make around money have an emotional component," she emphasizes, "but because this is unconscious, we aren't aware of how powerfully our emotions drive our behavior."

Still, most experts are quick to admit, these emotions about money are commonly suppressed, rarely explored, and little understood. "Psychology has just begun to unravel the mysteries of money," wrote Donald Katz in *Worth* magazine.

For women, the emotional component is particularly important to heed. Psychologist Kathleen Gurney developed a self-scoring financial profile, which she has given to more than fifty thousand people over the last decade. According to her findings, women experience more emotion and less confidence around money than men.

"A large number of these women were managerial and professional. They earned high incomes but had low accumulated wealth and the highest score in spending," Gurney told me. "Instead of dealing with their emotions, they were acting them out."

I'll never forget hearing a woman—I'll call her Sue—express her reaction to her inheritance. "I keep feeling maybe I should give this all away to someone who deserves it more," she cried. "I know it sounds irrational, but I don't feel I deserve it." For a long time, this woman could not, would not, take responsibility for her money.

This is not what most of us would expect. After all, money is supposed to solve problems, not create them. In fact, money is an extraordinary gift, but it's no panacea. And for many of us, unless we do the "inner work," money can become a virtual Pandora's box. "If you don't know who you are," economist Adam Smith once said, "the stock market is an expensive place to learn."

In other words, unless we deal with our unconscious attitudes, we will almost certainly sabotage our success. We can sabotage ourselves in all sorts of subtle ways. We'll neglect to balance our checkbook, misplace financial statements, overdraw our account, act impulsively, become too busy with other things, defer decisions indefinitely, or simply lose interest in anything related to money. These behaviors, like uninvited guests, show up without warning and, if ignored, may never leave.

I once had a very revealing conversation with a woman from a small midwestern town who was doing research for a book on inherited wealth. She had asked to interview me, and a few weeks after the interview, she sent me a transcript for my review. I could see immediately that this woman knew very little about finances. Clearly she did not understand any of the financial terms I had used—most of them were blatantly misspelled or entirely misused. I suggested to her, in a subsequent phone conversation, that she might want to educate herself before she tried to write a book to educate others.

Her response was a litany of excuses. "My parents never taught me. . . . I live in the boondocks. There is no one in this town who can help me . . . I tried to talk to my banker, but he didn't explain things clearly. . . . I have no time. I'm working on three different writing projects."

Her excuses, like my procrastination, kept our veils solidly intact. We each have our own ways of holding our veils in place. We rationalize, become disorganized, go stupid, fog up, or scare ourselves with what-ifs. Our methods may vary, but the reasons we engage in these behaviors are exactly the same. All veils are woven from virtually the same fabric—fear, that ubiquitous, penetrating, unrelenting emotion that obscures our perception like layers of gauze.

There wasn't a smart woman I interviewed who didn't mention fear at some point when discussing money. There is nothing inherently wrong with fear. It is a natural reaction to an unknown or a threatening situation. And without question, taking financial responsibility is, for many of us, a frightening, even ominous, unknown. Nevertheless, fear can play a positive role, alerting us to danger, preparing us for action. Like the brakes on a car, fear can keep us at a safe and reasonable speed.

"Fear has in some way motivated me to take my time, not act recklessly," Abby conceded during our interview.

But fear can backfire. Typically, when we're afraid of something, we want to avoid it. If we're afraid of making a mistake, losing money, or looking foolish, we're not apt to rush to the nearest stockbroker and demand that our money be put to work. More likely we won't go anywhere near a brokerage firm. Restraint is appropriate and advisable. Avoidance, however, only empowers the fear and produces anxiety.

When fear turns to anxiety, it narrows our vision, limits our choices, clouds our thinking, and reduces our ability to act, leaving us paralyzed, inert, and hopelessly stuck. Ironically, fear becomes a self-fulfilling prophecy, creating an environment ripe for whatever it is we fear most.

Lifting the Veils

How do we lift the veils, diminish our fear? The answer is simple, but it's not easy. Diminishing fear requires two steps:

- First, we need to figure out the source of our fear—by examining our beliefs around money.
- Second, we must take action—by doing the very thing we're afraid of doing.

Step One—Finding the Source of the Fear

Fear, like pain, is a symptom. If we probe deep enough, we will discover that our reaction to money mirrors our inner life and forecasts our outer life. Put another way, our fears reflect our beliefs, and our beliefs create our reality by governing our behavior. Self-deprecating beliefs lead to self-destructive behavior. "Believe you can. Believe you can't," Henry Ford once said. "Either way you'll be right." To take charge of our money in responsible ways may require a fundamental shift in our limiting beliefs.

BECOMING AWARE OF OUR BELIEFS

"Behavior can never go beyond beliefs," Ruth Hayden declares in *How to Turn Your Money Life Around*. How we act around money won't change without changes in what we believe—about money, about ourselves. Learning about money then becomes an *un*learning process as well. This unlearning is the very essence of the inner work we must do. Like a suit of clothes we've long outgrown, we must cast aside our old beliefs, our misguided attitudes, our distorted self-image as stupid, incompetent, incapable, needing to be rescued. Who we think we are stands in the way of who we want to be. The first step in lifting veils, then, is conscious awareness: becoming aware of our beliefs in regard to money.

"That's how we become unstuck," explains Abby during the course on women and money. "We become conscious of our money story. By looking at our past, we can unhook from it."

Our money story is the script we've concocted that establishes our role with money. This script is based almost exclusively on our beliefs and attitudes, which heavily influence our decisions and determine our direction. Beliefs may be powerful, but they are also arbitrary. Beliefs are simply decisions we've made based on emotional reactions to situations. Beliefs have no relationship to fact or reality.

Because they are made arbitrarily, they can be changed arbitrarily. First we must discover the source of our crippling beliefs. Next we'll learn how to change them. Our beliefs and attitudes toward money essentially stem from five different roots:

- our family messages
- our childhood experience
- prevailing cultural attitudes
- the source of our money
- the level of our self-esteem

Once we understand what our beliefs are and where they came from, we can replace them with new beliefs and write a new script. In an almost Zen fashion, we need to empty the container to fill it back up. Let's take a closer look at each of these five roots. As you read the following explanations, see if you can identify the beliefs that have become your stumbling blocks.

• FAMILY MESSAGES

Very often our financial difficulties can be traced directly to our parents' attitude toward money. Did Dad make all the decisions? Was Mom closemouthed about money? Were our parents raised in poverty or during the Depression? Did they stuff their savings under the mattress or spend every dime without thought? Were there unspoken rules about surpassing our family's economic status? As financial planner and psychologist Victoria Felton Collins told me, "Growing up during the breadlines is very different than being raised in the croissant age."

A successful businesswoman I once interviewed spoke candidly about her struggle to subdue her family's silent messages. "One of my issues has been that my family would not love me because I am financially successful," she told me. "Each time my life has notched up financially, that issue has come up for me. I worried that if I became wealthy, they wouldn't like me. I was afraid of losing them because I was going to be different." She sighed. "Rebelling against the course your family has charted for you is a very painful thing."

The members of our family were our earliest role models. Everything they did or said concerning money became a powerful message. We internalized those messages, and though they may be long forgotten, they still vigorously shape our behavior.

"My family had all these rules about 'You don't talk to people about money; you don't let people know what you've got,' " recalls Abby, who told me how hard it was for her to begin discussing money openly in her classes. What's more, she added, "There's a message in my family about money being scarce, about there never being enough, even though now I know that wasn't really true. But it's given me this sense of scarcity I can't shake, no matter how much I have."

• Childhood experiences

Other times, problems with money are symptoms of a gaping wound, a profound hunger, a desperate unhappiness rooted in childhood. In these cases, money may become both an anesthetic to numb the pain and a means of filling unmet needs. Both are impossible functions for money to perform and are inevitably doomed to fail. As the Beatles aptly put it, "Money can't buy me love."

Sue, who wanted to give her inheritance away, recalled being battered as a child. "When you're beaten, you feel like shit," she told me. "You know you're shit. They tell you you are shit. So when I got money, there was a feeling that would come over me, a change in my body, that maybe I'd better give this away because I wasn't deserving."

Audrey, who told us she made good money but had nothing to show for it, grew up in an alcoholic family. "In order not to deal with the pain of childhood," Audrey realized, "I'd spend and spend. I was so deprived as a child, I would insist I had to have certain things in my life. I would spend fifty dollars a week on flowers. If I couldn't sleep, I'd call the catalog people." But her spending only intensified, never eased, her pain. It was yet another way to remain a victim of her past. Not until she took control of her life, through counseling and twelve-step meetings, did she heal emotionally and financially.

• Cultural attitudes

We've spoken at length of the taboos and myths that say money is a man's concern and women need men to take care of them. We haven't mentioned the role religion has played. Many of us have been taught that money is "filthy lucre" and "the root of all evil." Yet our society covets affluence. Consequently, for some, wealth is something to be both revered and condemned. We admire the people who have it and resent them at the same time. Unless we are aware of this disparity in our thinking and find ways to resolve it (which we'll discuss later in this chapter), we may find ourselves in a financial conundrum. Unconscious ambivalence produces an internal conflict that can inadvertently reduce our monetary success.

- SOURCE OF THE MONEY

If our money was derived from tragedy, such as a debilitating accident, a painful divorce, or the death of a loved one, then our reaction to that money may be harshly colored by grief and intense emotion.

"I don't want my mother's money," I once heard a woman cry after her mother's death. "I want my mother."

If our money comes suddenly, hurling us unexpectedly into a new income bracket, then the transition can be difficult, inciting feelings of distrust, panic, and being different and alienated. "Coming into money can blast wide open your sense of self," says financial planner Amy Domini. Some psychologists say that receiving money can feel like a midlife crisis. The more extreme the change of class, the more difficult the adjustment. Interestingly, *U.S. News & World Report* reported that 80 percent of all millionaires come from middle- or working-class backgrounds.

It makes no difference how much money we have. Fear doesn't diminish. "If anything, the fear will increase," says Tracy Gary about the inheritors who call Resourceful Women for help. "Even if they have one or two million in the bank, there is a bag lady inside them. While their pockets may be deeper, their confidence isn't."

Particularly if a woman has never earned a living, she may have no confidence in her ability to support herself, and be terrified of making mistakes.

"What if I blow it?" claimed a woman about a small insurance settlement. "I know once it's gone, I can never get it back. I'm terrified of losing everything."

- OUR LEVEL OF SELF-ESTEEM

When you get right down to it, self-esteem is the most critical factor in financial success (or success in any endeavor).

"By the time I got money," a very savvy sixty-something inheritor told me, "I was married, had four kids, was successful in my career, and I felt good about myself." Not surprisingly, this woman had little trouble taking charge of her inheritance. My interviews definitely confirm that those women who expressed healthy levels of self-esteem were much more successful in handling money than those who were less self-assured.

Self-esteem is such a powerful force that unless we feel good about ourselves, we can easily hamstring our progress at every turn. Unless we feel strong, whole, and worthy, we're like a flimsy container that's too fragile to hold the money when it comes. Unfortunately, a lot of women find themselves in this predicament. A report by the American Association of University Women revealed that the level of girls' self-esteem drops by 50 percent between elementary school and high school.

I remember interviewing Karen McCall, now a nationally known financial counselor, who was once heavily in debt after she spent every penny of a substantial divorce settlement in less than two years.

"I never knew where it went," she lamented. "But I knew I had a very serious problem that had nothing to do with money. It had to do with my belief that I was no good and deserved no more."

Indeed, psychologists tell us that image precedes action. Actions, our behavior, show us what we think of ourselves. If we feel undeserving, we'll deplete our resources, no matter how much we have. If we think we're stupid, we'll fog up, or act "stupid," no matter how smart we are or how much we learn. But when we shift our self-image and change the way we view ourselves, our behavior will change to reflect the shift.

CHANGING BELIEFS

How do we shift our self-image, change our beliefs, and hence transform our behavior? How do we rise above distorted messages, heal our ancient wounds? A good friend, discussing her struggle to come to grips with her finances, told me, "The feeling that I should be taken care of was stronger than my belief I could do it myself. It was a subconscious internal conflict. But once I brought it to the surface and I was honest about what was going on internally, then I could confront the conflict and make choices."

Our task, then, and the real crux of the inner work, is to bring our internal conflicts and buried emotions to the surface. Women I interviewed reported choosing one or more of the following methods to accomplish this.

Some women, like myself, chose *psychotherapy*. "It's taken a year of therapy for me to abandon my family script," Sue, the woman who had been abused as a child, told me. "It was really wonderful to have someone to talk to. My parents had me so full of self-doubts. I'd wake up every morning and say, You can't do this. You're just Sue the dope. The therapist helped me see that though I've been battered, I am deserving. I saw the money was mine. I deserved it. Then I could face my financial responsibilities."

I had many women express similar sentiments. "Therapy helped me put it into perspective," said a middle-aged woman who, years ago, had behaved carelessly with money. "Just because I've blown it doesn't mean I can't fix it." Counseling need not be expensive. Many community mental health centers and individual therapists offer services based on sliding-scale fees.

Therapy certainly isn't the only option. Many women have great success with *support groups and classes*. These gatherings become a community, a place to verbalize our stories, and as Abby says, "the more we verbalize our stories, the more objective we can be." Managing Inherited Wealth (part of Resourceful Women) is such a support group for women. A member described their meetings: "We shared, we talked, we laughed. It was terribly freeing to have a place you could go, people you could talk to, where you could talk about problems, and people would understand those problems. They had been through similar things, and they could tell me what they'd tried and what worked and what didn't."

Carla, the struggling artist we met in the last chapter who inherited a small sum, attended Debtors Anonymous (DA), a twelve-step program like Alcoholics Anonymous. A friend urged her to attend a meeting when Carla first realized her excessive spending was depleting her inheritance. "Before you find yourself in debt," her friend warned, "get help."

Up until that first DA meeting, Carla remembered, "I was absolutely paralyzed and terrified about my money. I would wake up every morning with a knot in my stomach." But by talking aloud and listening to others, she identified the source of her anxiety and, in doing so, defused her fear. "I saw I had to let go of the way I saw myself and the world," she said. "I saw myself as this poor waif who didn't know how she was going to take care of herself. I also had to let go of the voice I got from my parents: I can't do that, I'm not good enough. They didn't say that in so many words, but it was what came across. Actually, when I started DA I considered myself involved in more important things, like art and creation. I had to come to terms with money as an important part of life, not to look down on it. Money isn't bad. It can allow me to live my spiritual values. It doesn't put me in a crass, competitive, nasty world." Carla's words beautifully describe the inevitable *unlearning* that will occur during the inner work.

Group experiences, however, aren't for everyone. And even if they work well for us, nothing can take the place of one-on-one discussions with people we know and trust. Most women found that *talking to friends* was enormously helpful.

Beth, a loan officer at a bank, told me she's been getting together with a friend once a month for the past two years. "He focuses on his money issues," she explained, "I focus on mine. We talk about our cash flow and balance sheets and where we are and what we want to create. It's great to have someone to bounce ideas off of."

But she quickly admits that in the beginning, this was one of the hardest things she ever did. She was deeply in debt and terribly ashamed. "When I first started sharing with him, I'd start crying because I was so embarrassed," she said, grimacing. "Being a banker, I thought I'd die if anyone knew I was in debt. Just looking at my money was humiliating. I felt like such a fraud. I had my money and my identity collapsed into one. That sharing alleviated a lot of the shame. Then it just started getting better. There was nothing to hide."

Abby herself is another example. When she realized psychological issues were at the root of her financial difficulties, she too turned to her friends. "I saw in some of my friends that they also got stuck in a money predicament. We started talking." From these conversations, she identified her problem. "I realized I had a belief that a man wouldn't want a woman who was smart with money," she said. Talking enabled her to break through this obsolete notion.

"Talking really helped," she told me. "For me, it was another way of breaking down the taboos. It brought my fear into consciousness, and listening to others, I didn't feel I was so weird. I realized others felt the same way. The more I talked, the more absurd the idea became. I had seen it so black and white: No man will love any woman with money, particularly

Abby. That may be true for some men, but it wasn't true for all men. This wasn't an absolute." As soon as she uncovered her psychological blocks, she was able to move on. "Money got simpler," she recalled. "I was willing to take more risks, try different investment vehicles. Managing money became so much easier."

Abby recently faced another hurdle, when she inherited a sizable amount of money from her parents. "In the last class I taught," she told me, "I realized I was feeling a distance between myself and the other women. I finally understood that I was embarrassed. I didn't want them to know I had money. When I had taught this class before my inheritance, I had felt equal. So I talked to them about it. I told them I didn't want to distance myself, but I was embarrassed to say I had money. A couple of others had the same feelings. They had inherited money and felt the same kind of barriers. It was a very powerful experience for everyone. But it was initially very hard for me to do. Since then, however, I am not as shy anymore about talking about money. I'm more open. It's becoming an integral part of who I am."

Talking, as Freud long ago discovered, can be the most effective remedy for what ails our psyche. Anytime we tell the truth, our emotional veils will begin to lift. Still, talking about money, even to our closest associates, is excruciatingly difficult for some of us. "People feel more ashamed around money problems than about sex and drugs," says financial counselor Karen McCall. "It is the last thing people really want to talk about."

If we can't talk to others, we can at least be honest with ourselves. Many women I interviewed described very private, often poignant moments of *personal soul searching* and self-discovery.

"I know that when I'm in fear it's time for me to write about it," a woman told me. "I spend a lot of hours writing. I look at where these fears come from. Is my fear in fact true? Am I going to run out of money? Or is this a past message from my parents about the work ethic?"

Marion told me that she once woke up in the middle of the night filled with frustration over her financial and professional life. "I sat down and made a list of all the obstacles that kept me from doing what I wanted. When I looked at the obstacles, it dawned on me that I could brainstorm how I planned to overcome each one. In other words, how I was going to empower myself. These obstacles were mine. The world wasn't doing it to me.

"Out of that, I began to take money more seriously. I paid off my debts. I opened a freedom account, an account that was going to set me free to start my own company. Once I got very intentional about what I wanted, things happened fast. It was really amazing. It was a process of learning how to trust myself." When she had a few months' savings, she began investing. Within two and half years she had her own business.

"For the first time in my life," Marion told me, after describing her middle-of-the-night revelations, "I truly made a commitment to myself, regardless of whether there was a man in my life or not. I realized I needed to shift the focus inward, from 'maybe I haven't found the right man' to 'I need to be the right person for myself.' So I got more committed to me."

Step Two—Taking Action: Doing What We Fear

Often, as we've seen in the above examples, merely identifying our internal barriers is enough to dissolve them, and the next step occurs easily, often automatically, even unexpectedly. Awareness can itself induce action. But not always. Sometimes, we have to push ourselves to take the next step, the step most of us have been trying our best to forestall. We must confront, head-on, whatever it is we fear. We must do the very thing we are most afraid to do. As Eleanor Roosevelt once said: "You gain strength, courage, and confidence by every experience in which you really look fear in the face."

"I always wondered if I chose to become a financial advisor because it would enable me to tackle my fears around money, since money was such an issue in my life," confessed a successful entrepreneur who grew up in poverty. "I never really articulated that before. But I suspect that on a deeper psychological level, I did this for a living like people who have had a lot of psychological problems become shrinks."

When it comes to finances (or anything else, for that matter), people fall into two categories—those who are afraid and take their fear with them and those who are afraid and let their fear stop them. Those in the first group become true heroines. They are the ones who become smart with money.

I remember a brochure that came in the mail advertising a personal growth workshop. I had no interest in the workshop, but the brochure grabbed my attention with these words: "Life is about handling higher levels of fear. So be willing to be scared and go where your fear is telling you. Because the very thing you're fearing now is the next door, is the door to enlightenment." Those words became the best financial advice I'd ever receive.

Those words also sum up the very essence of the hero's journey. All heroes must travel into the wilderness where they battle dragons, ward off demons, and suffer various frightening ordeals before returning to safety. "Always the path to return is to walk through fear," observed mythologist Joseph Campbell. The dragons we must face are our own fears personified. "All those dragon killings," he explained, "have to do with getting past being stuck." We kill the dragons by taking action.

I was deeply moved when Naomi, a very astute businesswoman, admitted she once suffered a devastating financial setback that left her literally broke. "How did you recover so beautifully?" I asked.

"I realized I couldn't be afraid anymore," she answered. "I realized there is always a course of action I can take. In the process of taking action, I healed myself. I was so clear: I just needed to take action. Not everything I did was correct action. But as long as I was in action . . ." Her voice trailed off. Then she said, "I think women forget that their actions are power. Any action you take is making a difference, moving the space around you. I think a lot of women don't take responsibility because they don't take action. If you're not out there taking action, you don't change anything."

What actions should we be taking? Any that initiate a momentum of dealing with money. Check the newspaper listings, then tune in to a financial talk show on the radio or television. Fill out a subscription to the *Wall Street Journal* and mail it. Stop by the newsstand, buy a *Smart Money* magazine, then read it that night. Pick up the phone, call the broker who gave last week's lecture, and make an appointment, then dial a friend and set up a lunch date to talk about investments.

One particularly enlightened broker, Ellen Stromberg, told me of a client who called her, saying, "Help! I don't know anything about money." Ellen asked the woman to come to her office. "She was in a whirlwind of confusion and couldn't get out," Ellen recalled. "We started by breaking everything down into small pieces. The first thing I had her do was just track her expenses, with no judgment. Then, when she understood her cash flow, she set goals. That helpless feeling began to disappear. So did her fears. She got to a place of power. Now, three years later, she calls me with investing ideas. Her helplessness is gone."

"Courage doesn't mean we're not afraid," Abby assured us as we sat in a circle that first day of class. "But we must be willing to act in spite of our fear. That's courage. The fact that you're here, sitting in this class, is a courageous act." Everyone nodded in agreement. "When we confront our resistance," she continued, "when we take action despite an unknown and uncertain future, that's courage."

This fear of an uncertain future is by far our biggest stumbling block. In a study of 4,200 women, the National Center for Women and Retirement Research found that fear of failure and the unknown, far more than lack of knowledge, were the greatest obstacles to women's financial success.

"All my life I was afraid of money," Renee admitted during our interview. "I'm still afraid. But now I say, okay, this is fear. I know that fear. I will do it anyway, and that fear will come with me. Fear doesn't seem to go away. It gets a little quieter occasionally. But it doesn't go away."

On the Far Side of Fear

Renee may be right. Fear may never completely go away. But invariably, each time we meet fear head-on and walk right through it, a gift awaits us on the other side. Beyond our fear lies our power, or, as Nietzsche wisely remarked, "That which does not kill us makes us stronger."

Money, we discover, becomes a forceful catalyst for our personal growth, and as a result, we may experience healing in other areas of our life as well. As we shed beliefs that thwarted our efforts to getting smart with money, we inevitably become more of who we were meant to be. "Our relationship with money can be a potent instrument in our search for self-knowledge," wrote philosopher Jacob Needleman. And, we could easily add, a mighty implement in our pursuit of self-esteem. Just as self-esteem influences the way we handle money, financial aptitude affects our self-esteem.

"When women do reckon with their attitudes and feelings about money," says psychologist Kathleen Gurney, "what I see is a tremendous amount of self-confidence and a real boost in self-esteem."

Many of the women I interviewed said the same. "It has been empowering in ways far beyond anything I could have imagined," exclaimed Carla. "I am not just talking about the nuts and bolts of finances. I am talking about my self-image and self-confidence." And another woman laughed as she said, "It's done more for me than losing twenty pounds."

Self-confidence is an essential ingredient in the recipe for financial success. Like yeast to bread, without it we'll never rise above our habitual behaviors or the herd mentality. As we gain more confidence in ourselves, we'll begin to trust our judgment. We will be less likely to remain rooted in fear or to blindly follow the masses. This is when we'll begin to grasp the next realization. Behind the veils of fear lie the real "secrets" of financial success.

Now we're ready for the outer work.

⋯ CHAPTER FIVE RECAPPED ⋯

Realization: If we have trouble learning about money or acting on what we learn, as many of us do, then it's time to turn inward, examine our emotional blocks, change our fallacious beliefs, and conquer our inhibiting fears.

To Do
1. Try this exercise to help focus inward:

Quickly complete these sentences with the first word(s) that come to your mind. It's not important to be right; it's more important to respond quickly, without much thought. This exercise is a way of unlocking doors to your inner self. In fact, some of your responses might surprise you.

- My mother felt money was _____
- My father felt money was _____
- Growing up, I considered money to be _____
- My greatest fear concerning money is _____
- I believe money should be _____
- Sometimes, I sabotage myself financially by _____
- If I gave my "money story" a title, it would be _____
- Financially, I keep feeling I should _____
- Money brings me joy because _____
- Money creates anxiety for me because _____

2. Your responses to this sentence-completion exercise can be revealing. What do your findings tell you? Did you uncover any clues to your difficulties? Did you discover issues you need to resolve? Did the exercise trigger any additional thoughts? Work with your insights. Talk about your attitudes toward money, any fears you may have, with a friend or therapist, or write in a journal, meditate, whatever feels most comfortable.

3. Read *Money Is My Friend*, by Phil Laut, a wonderful, insightful little book that has become a classic. Another good one is *Unbalanced Accounts: How Women Can Overcome Their Fear of Money*, by Annette Lieberman and Vicki Linder.

Chapter Six

• •

Realization #4:
There Are No Secrets

Q: Why did God create economists?
A: To make weather forecasters look good.

No one knows what the economy is going to do. No one can predict with 100 percent accuracy how various markets will perform, when financial fluctuations will occur, or which stock or mutual fund will be tomorrow's winner or loser. "Even the experts aren't so expert," asserted a recent *Wall Street Journal* headline. But how many of us discount our own opinions in favor of an "expert" cited in the newspaper? How many of us believe these purported experts have a corner on the truth, that they're privy to certain well-kept secrets? How many of us think that until we figure out what those secrets are, we'd better not do anything at all?

I'll always remember a conversation I overheard during a seminar lunch break. The woman sitting next to me was telling two friends across the table about her naive entry into the investment world.

"I knew that if I invested the money wisely I could make more money," this woman was saying, "but I didn't know how one invested wisely. I kept thinking that smart people did certain things. Like there was a list of secrets that these people knew, and I just needed to find somebody who would give me the list. Then I'd be okay."

"I wish there were some great wisdom that would tell me what I should do," sighed another. "But you realize no one really knows. Not stock-brokers, not money managers."

"Listen, I work in investments," the third woman chimed in. "I see that nobody really knows what the market is going to do. There are no secrets in this business."

The first woman laughed. "Yeah, I know that now. I've learned that most people don't know anything about investing, and they go ahead and do it anyway. They look like they know what they're doing, but they don't."

These women had come to a crucial realization. *There are no secrets.* No one has a magic formula for financial success. "In investments, as in many other areas, very few people really know what they are talking about—and the rest is just conversation," observed a columnist for the *International Herald Tribune*. Of all the women I've interviewed, not one alluded to privileged information or arcane facts. What they spoke of was a long learning curve, a lot of stop and go, and unswerving determination. The whole idea of financial secrets is not only foolish; it can be detrimental to our financial future.

The Myth of Financial Secrets

When we think there are mysteries to managing money, and we don't know what they are, we become unsure of ourselves, afraid to make choices, unable to act. According to Esther Berger, author of *Money Smart*, chronic financial paralysis among women "has been created and perpetuated, generation after generation, by the belief that financial know-how involves secret, mysterious knowledge intrinsic to men, that there are, in fact, money secrets men never tell women."

The sooner we realize there are no secrets, the faster our progress will be. Unfortunately, this aura of mystery thrives in a culture where economists are touted as prophets who can foresee the future, where market commentators become gurus uttering irrefutable truths, where today's hottest money managers are followed like cult leaders with celebrity status. Their words cast long, dark shadows over our own trifling opinions.

"Stock stars are treated like rock stars," Peter Lynch quips in his must-read book *Beating the Street*. This kind of veneration, he writes, "gives the amateur investor the false impression that he or she couldn't possibly hope to compete against so many geniuses with MBA degrees."

Nothing could be further from the truth, and to prove it, Lynch relates "The Miracle of St. Agnes." St. Agnes is a school whose seventh-grade class put together a group of stocks that gained a whopping 70 percent in two years. These twelve-year-olds surpassed 99 percent of all professional equity mutual fund managers. An inspiring story, to be sure, but really no miracle. It's a well-known fact that 80 percent of all financial advisors can't keep pace with the overall market. I once attended a financial planning seminar at which the instructor looked directly into the audience and told us point-blank: "You people sitting in this room have a better chance of beating the market than professional money managers." At the time, I thought he was crazy. But now I know he is right.

Consider the *Wall Street Journal*'s infamous stock-picking contest. Every quarter, three financial experts compete against a dartboard to see who names the best-performing stock. Guess what wins the overwhelming majority of times? Now, if a bunch of prepubescent kids and a random dart can make money in the market, we can surely do as well.

Not only are the experts often off target, but they charge outrageous fees for their inferior performances. *Fortune* magazine, in a cover story, rebuked the majority of money managers because even though they deliver poor results, they have the fastest-growing profit margins in any United States industry.

That doesn't mean we shouldn't seek assistance from financial professionals. It simply says we must watch them like a hawk. We can't assume they've got all the answers. The truth is, just because someone has an MBA, works on Wall Street, or is quoted in the press, it doesn't mean he or she has an infallible grip on the future.

John Kenneth Galbraith likes to say, "There are two types of economic forecasters. Those who don't know and those who don't know they don't know." The financial press is full of examples. For instance, on October 11, 1987, the chief strategist for Prudential Bache assured clients that "despite the general uneasiness in the market ... nothing bad will occur." That same day, a popular financial newsletter, *Standard and*

Poor's Outlook, promised readers in bold letters, "Peak not yet in sight." The folks who made decisions based on those rosy predictions probably kicked themselves afterward. Two days later, the market plummeted 190 points, the second-biggest drop in history. Citing examples like this, the editors of *Money* magazine posed an interesting question: If Wall Street professionals can be so "badly blindsided, what chance do individuals stand?" Their answer: "Better than you think."

As financial columnist Herb Greenberg counsels readers, "You should take what you read, see and hear not with a grain of salt, but an entire salt shaker full. If we business journalists were such geniuses, we would all be out making money for ourselves playing the market, not digging up information for you."

No one—whether amateur or professional—has any special secrets for financial success, but most investors who have done well in the market have acquired some sensible bits of wisdom that have held them in good stead.

Beyond Secrets: Words to the Wise

Later during the seminar at which I overheard the conversation at lunch, I made a point of finding the woman who had sat next to me. "I'm just curious," I told her, admitting I had eavesdropped. "How did you finally realize there was no list of secrets?"

She laughed, then took a moment to ponder my question. "I guess it was by talking to people," she answered. "I especially remember a friend I really respected. She assured me there was no such list. She said that there were certain things that people need to do in order to protect themselves. But there is no universal list of best things to do, because everyone is different. This made sense to me."

This woman had made an important discovery. While there is no list of secrets, there are "certain things" smart investors do. In the often confusing financial arena, many investors have come to rely on a body of wisdom that has been passed down over the years, usually from father to son, from one man to another. This body of wisdom consists of "certain things" people can do to protect their assets and augment their wealth. In truth, these are nothing more than commonsense rules of thumb that smart people either instinctively know or (more likely) eventually learn.

Women, long denied opportunities to handle money, have generally been deprived of this information as well. The more women learn about money, the more we're apt to pick up these "things" on our own—not secrets, but for lack of a better phrase, let's call them words to the wise. Though definitely not a definitive list, the words to the wise most often mentioned during my interviews can be summed up in the following seven tenets:

- Trust your intuition
- Learn from your mistakes
- Go slow
- Start small
- Invest regularly
- Diversify broadly
- Know what you're buying

• *Trust your intuition*

> *"The really valuable thing is intuition."*
> —*ALBERT EINSTEIN*

I once asked Margaret, a business school graduate and an active investor, what she attributed her financial success to. "It wasn't anything I read in a book," she explained. "It was more from my own gut." Listening to our intuition, trusting our feelings, is a major factor in financial success. The smart women I spoke to didn't ignore external data, nor did they rely solely on their instincts. They checked out their hunches by doing their homework. They listened to the experts, acquired the facts, completed the learning curve. They became knowledgeable enough to make in-formed choices. But when it came to making a final decision, they trusted themselves. They came to recognize that their internal radar was as trust-worthy as any expert's opinion.

The notion of women's intuition isn't hype. When we trust our hunches, we're generally right. Like exercising a muscle, the more we use our intuition, the stronger it becomes. "My intuition never fails me." the Sufis say, "but I fail when I fail to listen to it."

Most women I interviewed told me they made their worst mistakes when they didn't follow their better judgment. (The second-largest cause of mistakes was not doing their homework.) Frances was one of these women. Displaying the sophisticated flair of someone who grew up in a well-to-do family, Frances spoke poignantly about her desperate efforts to take financial control. "In the beginning, my impulsiveness and my fear working together were really a disaster," she told me. "I didn't know very much. I'd get a good idea. I'd invest. The stock would go down or I would read something bad about it in the paper, then I would get out. I always lost money. My fear made it harder for me to get back in."

She gave me an example, which occurred around the time Congress was voting on whether to ratify the North American Free Trade Agreement (NAFTA), which would, among other things, encourage commerce between the U.S. and Mexico. "I had this Telmex stock," she recalled, referring to the Mexican telephone company. "I knew it would do well if NAFTA passed. And I just knew NAFTA was going to pass. Yet I picked up the *Wall Street Journal*, and one expert after the other said Telmex was not going to do well, it had had its day, so get rid of it. I put down the *Journal*, got on the telephone, and called the broker, who agreed I should sell the stock, and I did. Of course, it went up about fourteen points. Why did I do that? I wondered."

Why had she? "I had no confidence in myself," she admitted.

But it was a lesson well learned. "I started to learn more, talk to more people, research my ideas," she told me. As she became better educated, she was more "emboldened." Now, when she talks to her broker, "I don't always do what he says. I realize it's my choice." And by her own admission, she's done quite well by trusting her choices.

• *Learn from your mistakes*

> *"Mistakes: without them life would be dull."*
> —OSCAR WILDE

The collective wisdom we're talking about has evolved essentially from one source—people's mistakes. We can't eliminate all mistakes by following these folks' hard-won wisdom, but we can certainly minimize their impact, possibly decrease their occurrence, and hopefully cut our financial losses. When it comes to learning any skill—whether it's investing or crocheting—mistakes are unavoidable. They're certainly part and parcel of investing. Still, Oscar Wilde's statement notwithstanding, no one in her right mind wants to make a mistake with her money. We're dealing not just with dollars but with our sense of security.

As one inheritor told me, "If you've never earned much money and have no hope of ever earning that much, then mistakes can feel a lot more serious." It's true, a bad mistake can be extremely costly. But avoiding mistakes can be even costlier. Yet the majority of women are trying to do just that. In its survey of 4,200 women, NCWRR found that 54 percent postponed financial decisions for fear of making a mistake. Such passivity can have irreparable consequences.

Frances, for example, told me that after her father died, he left her mother with a sizable estate. Both Frances and her mother, who "knew zilch," were afraid to take charge, so they handed the entire estate over to the trusted family lawyer, an old friend of her father's. Too late, Frances realized that this trusted lawyer had grossly mismanaged their money.

"When my mother died, fifty percent of her estate went out the window," Frances said ruefully. "The lawyer took gigantic fees. We got totally socked with taxes. It was a whole line of mismanagement. All that my father worked so hard for went into the lawyer's pocket or the government's hand. I keep thinking of all the ways I could have used that money for good causes. It's so hard to look back."

Today Frances considers that incident a painful but significant lesson. "It started me thinking about these things," she says, crediting that fiasco with her determination to get smart. She still makes mistakes, but none has ever cost her so dearly. And though she doesn't relish making them, over time she's come to realize that mistakes have been her best teachers. "I've learned from every mistake I've made," she told me.

Still, she admits, her first mistakes were agonizing. Many of us can relate to that feeling. Problem is, the people we look to as role models and rely on as experts rarely talk about their bloopers.

Frances told me how "humiliated" she felt when her first major invest-ment failed miserably—a gym that went bankrupt. "The first thing I thought was thank God my father was dead and not here to see this," she said. "I never heard about mistakes my father made. We only heard of his brilliant decisions, how he'd outsmarted the market, his wonderful intui-tion, how he knew when the market was going to go up. It was like my father was this mythical character who excelled in the real world."

Truly, only a mythical character (or a liar) has never made a mistake in the market. Mistakes are not only inevitable, they can, as Frances pointed out, be invaluable teachers. "You're never a good investor until you make a bad mistake," Michael Smith, a money manager, once told me. I think he's right. There wasn't one person I spoke to who didn't refer to a big blunder as a priceless lesson, an essential part of her learning curve.

Margaret, for example, was a vivacious, newly married, young businesswoman. I'll never forget the story she told me about her very first investment in the mutual fund Twentieth Century Ultra. "In October I bought Ultra at $15 a share," she recalled. "I put my whole savings in it, and every month I added $300. Then I looked at it every single day. Every single day my husband would hear me yelling from the other room because the fund was going down. Then in February it dropped to $12.75 a share. I panicked and sold it all at a loss."

Since she sold it, the fund has soared. Today Ultra is worth over $21 a share. "I don't own it anymore," Margaret said. "Had I just sat tight, I would have been fine. I learned a lot from that. You don't look at the fund every day. You do not sell at the low. And you don't put all your money in one place."

That one mistake taught Margaret, who had an MBA, about investing in a way that no textbook ever did. Her story taught me a lot too. (Another word to the wise: We can learn as much from other people's mistakes as we can from our own.) Coincidentally (or perhaps it was the luck of the learning curve), right before I interviewed Margaret, I had purchased shares in Ultra. It was one of my first investments. And as it had for Mar-garet, no sooner had I bought it than it started going down. Watching it nosedive was making me nervous, and I was ready to dump it. But after listening to Margaret, I stayed put. It didn't make sense to sell purely on fear when the facts pointed in a different direction (another word to the wise). Nothing had changed, so far as the fund was concerned. It still had the same manager who had been responsible for its stellar performance over the years. The prospectus had warned investors this would be a volatile fund, meaning it would go up and down a lot over time. Sure enough, the fund bounced back, and as of today, though it's been a bumpy ride, I still own it.

There is something else to consider. While it's important to learn from mistakes, we can't let ourselves dwell on them. "What's a mistake?" Naomi responded when I asked about hers. "You do the best you can do at the time. We think we made a good decision if our stock goes up and a bad decision if it doesn't. But it's not a matter of good and bad. There are all kinds of things we can't control. We pick a good stock—who is to know the company's president is going to abscond with all the money? Our decision was a good one. That's how I have to look at it. Otherwise, I'd make myself crazy when things don't work out."

Unfortunately, many of us aren't so generous with ourselves. Instead we beat ourselves up for not being perfect. I am reminded of a friend who recently made a chunk of money selling a book, yet was constantly berating herself for not doing more and advancing faster in terms of her finances.

"But look how far you've come," I reminded her. "You never had money before, and suddenly you have it. You've paid off your debts. You've chosen an investment advisor. You've set up a Keogh plan. You've worked through a zillion issues with your husband."

But she refused to acknowledge her progress. Like many women, she had an unrealistic standard of perfection, and when she didn't reach it, she felt like a failure. Margaret told me she had done the same thing until she realized how detrimental it was. "If we expect perfection, which I did for a long time, it's a no-win situation," she told me. "I didn't feel good about the things I did, because I wanted them to be perfect. If we wait until we're perfect and we have all the answers, we'll never get anywhere."

Brooding over our imperfections can interfere with our achievements. If we see only our mistakes, we may miss our successes. Plus, when we focus exclusively on what we haven't done, we are sending a message to our brain that says we're not in control and we're not up to the task. Remember, our attitudes and beliefs, more than anything else, shape our behavior and determine the outcome. Better to magnify small successes than focus heavily on our failures.

Ironically, my friend who had made money on the sale of her book had no idea how smart she actually was to go slow. She didn't realize that she had inadvertently stumbled onto another bit of wisdom for financial success: The best way to reduce the likelihood of error is to take your time. Any financial advisor worth a fee would tell her the same thing.

• *Go slow*

> *"Be not afraid of going slow, be only afraid of standing still."*
>
> —*CHINESE WISDOM*

"Go slow," Dick Schindler, a friend and financial advisor, once counseled me when I began rushing to get a handle on investing. "There is no hurry. Build confidence. Develop a comfort level."

Even as I became more savvy, others gave me similar advice. I once met with investment advisor John Harriman. Even though he wanted my account, he urged me to take my time. "Don't let anyone pressure you," he warned me. "Don't let anyone tell you you have to invest today or tomorrow or right this minute. There is always another stock, always another chance."

Of course, not everyone is so noble. There are hordes of zealous professionals, eager for our business, who will push us in another direction. To them, we're not a person but a potential commission. I've had a number of them admonish me for wasting time and losing money. One stockbroker warned me that if I didn't buy what he recommended on the spot, I'd miss out on an unprecedented, never-to-come-again opportunity. Another, badgering me to make a decision, must have asked me a dozen times, "So when are you going to decide? What are you waiting for?"

Fortunately, I wasn't bullied by their pressure tactics, especially when, in hindsight, I see how off-base their advice was. I am convinced that in the money game, slow but steady wins the race, provided, of course, we're advancing and not standing still.

"It's taken a long time. I went really slow," said Wendy, a young single mother, describing her financial evolution. "I think I had a lot of fear of making a mistake in the beginning. But it's been seven years, and I haven't lost my money. It's been a process. I feel very competent in terms of taking care of it. I think part of the process has been finding out I am not an idiot, realizing I've done okay with myself. I haven't shot myself in the foot. The most important thing for me to learn was to go slow and it's okay."

"I have a rule of thumb," financial planner Ginger Applegarth, author of *The Money Diet*, tells her clients. "Give yourself one week for every year of your life to change your money behavior." We're changing years of conditioning, she warns. This takes time.

Novice investors, however, are rarely long on patience. Most beginners I have observed tend to fall into one of two camps—either they become totally paralyzed or they get terribly impulsive. For those of us in the second group, going slow can be pure torture. We're impatient for instant results and berate ourselves harshly for less than immediate action. It's part of that ideal standard we've manufactured in our heads. I remember having lunch with two friends, one of whom was very distressed. "My mother died and left me a pretty big inheritance," she told us, "but I still have it sitting in a passbook savings account. I used to work at a bank. I should know better." She took a deep breath and continued. "I'm so afraid I can't trust myself. I've heard that people go through windfalls in five years. I'm afraid I won't think this through."

"When did you get the money?" my other friend asked.

"Two weeks ago." She sighed.

"Give yourself time!" we cried in unison, both of us assuring her she was doing the right thing.

She wasn't being negligent. She was being responsible, taking time to get her bearings and think things out. Patience is particularly important when money comes suddenly, unexpectedly, or tragically. It's tough to think clearly under those circumstances. Whatever our situation, we need to develop a game plan. Our financial decisions will depend on various factors: How much money do we have? What do we need our money for? (Retirement? Our kids' college? A new house?) When do we need our money? (Ten years? Five years? Next summer?) Whether we invest for the long term or the short term will greatly influence the choices we make.

This is where a financial planner can be helpful (as we will discuss in Chapter Eight). Investing is not something we want to do willy-nilly.

"It took me over a year before I got my entire estate invested," said a woman who inherited about $250,000 from an aunt and immediately sought help from a financial planner. "I loved planning my investments. It took months, looking at all the what-ifs, all the ways to protect my estate."

Following in the footsteps of the women I interviewed, I crept at a snail's pace. It took an entire year, from the time I started my self-education program, before I made my first investment. And it took another full year to become fully invested. I was too chicken to dive in headfirst and smart enough to know better. I first figured out exactly how much I would invest and where I would invest it, then I developed a schedule for investing. I did "dollar cost averaging": Instead of investing the lump sum in one fell swoop, I put in a small amount of money every month. I had uncovered another word to the wise.

• Start small, invest regularly, and diversify broadly

> *"Don't put all your eggs in one basket."*
> —PROVERB

Part of going slow is starting small. As one woman told me, when she decided to invest some of her savings, she kept her money where it was, in a money market fund, and, instead of charging ahead thoughtlessly, began to bone up on finances. "I did some reading, and then I found a broker," she said. "I gave him $10,000. That was a hefty sum, but if I lost it, my kids could still go to college. We invested it a little bit at a time in three different funds." This was indeed a smart woman.

I interviewed another woman who turned a few thousand dollars into a six-figure portfolio with some pretty daring investments.

"You're very bold," I exclaimed.

"Only with chunks of it, Barbara," she quickly replied. "I'm willing to be bold with chunks, but not all."

If, like these women, we invest only whatever amounts we can afford to lose and spread our money among different investment vehicles, the results of any bad decision won't be so jarring. Especially if we're new to the investment game, trial and error is part of our education. As Linda Pei of Women's Equity Mutual Fund often tells people, "It doesn't make any difference how little it is—you are investing in yourself. When you put in a little money, you learn how it works. Ultimately the real value is your own knowledge."

Margaret's big mistake, when she bought shares in Ultra, was to dump her entire nest egg in only one fund. "I put in $2,500—which was all my savings," she recalled. "I never had savings before." No wonder she panicked.

The next time around, she took a different approach—going slow and starting small. "I picked three funds I thought were really good, and I studied them. I did a little spread sheet, and I'd track the price every day without putting my money in. That was in February. In October I starting putting a little bit of money in each one every month."

As Margaret learned from her Ultra debacle, "You don't put all your money in one place. You diversify." Diversification means dividing your eggs (money) into different baskets (investments). By diversifying, we protect ourselves from staggering losses. According to the "Rule of Five," in any group of five investments, one will be a loser, three will be mediocre, and one will exceed all expectations. This one winner will more than offset the losers or laggards.

What's more, investment categories behave differently. Each asset class—stocks, bonds, cash, real estate, and perhaps commodities—normally responds differently to different market conditions and economic trends. When stocks go up, bonds tend to maintain their value. The same holds true for different categories within each class and different industries within each category. When foreign markets are sinking, domestic markets could be soaring. Smaller companies often perform differently than large ones. High-tech companies may be in vogue when, say, banks are out of favor. There are exceptions; this is not a hard-and-fast rule. But if we spread our money among various investments, and one goes down, another will likely go up. If, on the other hand, all our money is in, let's say, our company stock and that stock takes a tumble, we could be in serious trouble. It may be a perfectly good company. But even the best businesses have been battered by a troubled market or faltering industry.

"Seventy-five percent of the change in stocks will happen because of the movement of the overall market, not the particular company," John Morre, a financial planner, once explained to me. "All securities tend to follow market ups and downs." He and every other financial counselor promote the idea of a diversified portfolio, with a variety of investments in different markets and asset classes.

I vividly remember my conversation with Myra, a powerhouse real estate agent, who was dressed in an exquisite bright-red designer suit when we met. "I don't have the time to read about investment stuff or shop around trying to find what has the highest yield," she told me. "To me, in the time it would take to study the stocks, it would be just as easy to go sell a couple more houses."

No surprise, she buys only real estate. "Single-family homes," she said. "I rent them out. Or I buy and sell. I have done very well. I also loan money. I have since 1982, when the prime was high and some of my clients borrowed from me when they bought properties from me. I help them, and I get a good return on my money. It turned out to be a profitable thing."

Up to now, Myra has done well. But what if the real estate market hit bad times, as it has before and will again? Myra could be in the same kind of trouble as another real estate agent I interviewed. "In 1982 the real estate market crashed," she reminded me. "That same year, my back went out and I couldn't work for ten months. It was very scary. I lost a lot of money. But it was an eye-opening experience. I started looking at investing very differently."

Her story serves as a cautionary tale on the value of diversifying before we're caught in a bind. As the saying goes, it wasn't raining when Noah built the ark. Remember, *we don't need a lot of money to put together a diversified portfolio*. Mutual funds have become immensely popular for this reason. When we buy a mutual fund, we are pooling our money with other people's money, to buy a varied list of stocks, bonds, or whatever investment the particular fund emphasizes. We become a small investor with a large, diversified portfolio managed by a professional. As of this writing, there are at least sixteen no-load funds (funds without a sales charge) that have outstanding records, lower-than-average fees, and monthly minimums as low as $100, some even as low as $25 on an automatic investment plan. And if we can't afford to make the maximum contribution to our 401(k), we can put in as little as one percent of our paycheck.

Miriam is a grandmotherly sort, whose eyes sparkled with delight when she told me how she grew her $5,000 initial investment into $50,000. "I spread my money around, and it's done extremely well," she proudly explained, "because in any one year, if one or two stocks go down, the others go up. I didn't get badly hit in the 1987 [stock market] crash."

Besides diversification, the key to financial success can be described in one word: compounding. Perhaps the most powerful component in creating wealth, compounding means we earn money on our earnings as well as our original investment. Einstein called compounding the "greatest mathematical discovery of all time." To reap the rewards of compounding requires very little effort on our part—all we need to do is keep adding to our investments.

By automatically transferring a fixed sum from our paycheck or bank account to our investment account, and reinvesting any dividends or capital gains, we will accumulate a surprisingly sizable portfolio. Especially if we start at an early age. The longer our time frame, the greater the financial gain.

Here is an example of how compounding works. Say we'd like to retire by age sixty-five with $1 million. And let's say our investments earn 8 percent a year. If we wait until we're forty-five to start investing, we'll have to sock away some $21,900 a year. But if we begin at age twenty-five, we'll only need to put in $3,900 a year.

For those women still in their twenties, this is really great news. But what about those of us well over forty? Or even sixty? What do we do? According to Eastern philosophy, "The best time to plant a tree is twenty years ago. The next-best time is today." Regardless of our age, today is the best time to start investing small amounts on a regular basis. Keep in mind, a sixty-year-old most likely has decades left to enjoy life, compound her money, and secure her future.

• *Know what you're buying*

> *"Never invest in an idea you can't illustrate with a crayon."*
>
> —PETER LYNCH

How do we know which investments to select? This is where many of us are sure there is some big, dark secret. Linda Pei was a college student and recent Chinese immigrant with a few hundred dollars in the bank when she walked into a brokerage firm and asked the first broker she saw that question. The broker answered her question with a question: "What are you interested in?" Linda, an avid bike rider, told him bicycles. "He looked up all the bicycle companies, and we went through each one," Linda recalled. "We bought Schwinn. I made a lot of money from that."

Linda learned an important fact for successful stock picking—know what you're buying. She still follows the same tactic today, buying only those companies she understands and that sound interesting. "Unfortunately, more brokers don't take this approach," she said. "If you're interested in it, you are more likely to do the research and learn about the company."

Remember Anne Schreiber, the government worker we met in the Introduction, who made $22 million from a $5,000 initial investment? Her strategy was simple. She invested only in companies she understood. "She was a real movie fan," her stockbroker, William Fey, told *Winning Strategies* magazine. So along with big names like Pepsi-Cola and Coca-Cola, movie studio stocks were a core part of her portfolio. "She just kept buying more and more shares of the companies she knew and liked," said Fey, explaining that his client rarely bought more than 100 shares at a time. (And then she held on to them, regardless of what the market did. More about that approach in the next chapter.)

Mary Rodas is another example of how this works. Mary was written up in the *New York Times* for her stock-picking prowess. Her secret was no more than common sense. "I picked Disney because I grew up with it," she told the *Times*. "I picked General Electric because I remember the light-bulbs Dad put in the lamps in the building where he was the superintendent. Hershey? Every time I'm in the drugstore, I grab a Hershey bar.

Once I was having some Luden's and I turned the box over. That's how I found out it's a Hershey company too, so Hershey does great in the winter—all those cough drops."

By the way, Mary is seventeen years old. Her logic was impeccable, but only a starting point. Before we buy a stock, no matter how well known the name, we need to check it out. How does it compare to its competitors? What risks are associated with this firm? What are its prospects for future growth? Likewise, if we're considering mutual funds or a money manager, we need to familiarize ourselves with the people in charge. How have they done in up and down markets? What degree of risk do they normally take? What is their investment style and fee structure? There are a zillion questions we need to ask. And there are resources like *Value Line* (for individual stocks) and *Morningstar* (for mutual funds) that have the information we need. These guides, which can be found in most libraries, will tell us everything we need to know about a particular company or mutual fund.

I remember asking Margaret how she picked her three funds out of the thousands available. "I had some criteria," she explained, "specific things I was looking for. I wanted all no-loads. I would never, ever pay a fee for somebody's beautiful headquarters. The fund manager had to be there for five years. It took *me* five years to learn my job and do it well. I also wanted good returns. I was a comptroller at a bank, so I knew about returns. And I wanted the fund to do much better in a one-year bracket than a three-year bracket. I think it's harder to do well over a longer period of time. So in three years, it doesn't have to beat the S&P index by 10 percent, it only has to beat it by eight percent. Then in five years, it only has to beat it by three percent. I just gave it a little bit of a break, the longer I had to measure it."

Figuring out the right questions, finding the answers, and determining our criteria is part of what we discover during our time on the learning curve. Just as it's important to buy what we know, the opposite holds true. When we don't understand something, then we shouldn't invest in it, regardless of what experts or even friends tell us. If, after we do our homework, we are still puzzled, then maybe that is a sign we had better look elsewhere.

"If you don't understand an investment, odds are that it may not be right for you," writes Eric Tyson in his highly readable *Personal Finance for Dummies*. "You don't need to understand your investment well enough to become a financial counselor, but you should know the track record of the investment, its true costs, and how legitimate it is."

Frances can vouch for that bit of wisdom. She talked about her first investment, the gym that had gone belly up. "I jumped into something I didn't know anything about," she lamented. "I had no idea what it entailed to run a gym. I just liked to work out. When it went bankrupt, I remember the humiliation I felt."

"As far as I'm concerned, a risky investment is something I don't understand," declared financial consultant Joyce Linker. "I understand the stock market. For me, investing in the market is appropriate. But I don't understand real estate."

She recalls attending a presentation for a real estate project with her husband. "All our friends were putting their money in," she said. "But I told my husband, 'I don't understand it; I just don't get it. And I am smart. I understand stuff. Why don't I get it?' It turned out that it was a bad project, a strip shopping center that gave these friends of ours nothing but aggravation."

Now That We're Clued In to Market Wisdom, What's Next?

We have come a long way in our discussion of money. We know we need to take the financial reins because no one will do it for us. We also understand there is a learning curve to travel and a certain amount of overwhelm we must wade through. If we get stuck, we recognize that we may need to look inside to find the way out. And now we've come to see there are no secrets, only smart things that smart people do. If we liken money to swimming, we could say this: Here we are, standing at the edge, poised to dive in. We take a deep breath . . . and gulp! Suddenly the financial seas look awfully scary. The stock market, like the surf, seems choppy and unstable. What if something happens? After all, even the best and brightest have gone under. Sure they tell us that amateurs stand as good a chance of doing well as the pros. Right now, though, we wonder. Is the risk worth it? The reason we're so reticent is because we haven't learned an important lesson—how to stay afloat in treacherous financial waters. Once we grasp the following realization, we'll understand that the turbulence may not be as dangerous as it seems.

··· CHAPTER SIX RECAPPED ···

Realization: There is nothing mysterious about investing, nor is there *one right way* to get smart with money. There are, however, certain elements common to every success story. If we trust our intuition, learn from our mistakes, go slow, start small, diversify broadly, and invest regularly and knowledgeably, we'll become our own financial experts.

To Do
(Note: The purpose of these "To do's" is to familiarize yourself with the market, not necessarily to take action. If you're already investing actively, use this list to reevaluate your current holdings, research new ideas, or explore asset classes you might not be familiar with, such as bonds, commodities, REITs, international or sector funds.)

1. Pick a few businesses that you are familiar with. They can be anything from a restaurant—say, McDonald's—to a favorite store, like The Gap, to the car you drive, perhaps Ford. Find out if these are publicly listed companies. Follow the companies' stocks in the newspaper, writing down their daily or weekly closing prices. Do this for several months. (You can do the same with mutual funds.)

2. Try researching these companies by reading reports on them in *Value Line*; for mutual funds, refer to *Morningstar*. Both these publications contain one-page, detailed descriptions of virtually thousands of stocks or mutual funds. They can be found in your local library or any brokerage firm. (Warning: The information may appear overwhelming if you don't understand how it is organized. Both publications have an instructional guide. If you're not familiar with these publications, study the instructions. Or find someone to explain them to you.)

3. Read the *Wall Street Journal's Guide to Understanding Personal*

Finance, by Kenneth M. Morris and Alan Siegal. This is a wonderful primer for beginners and a great review for the more sophisticated. *Understanding Wall Street*, by Jeffrey Little and Lucien Rhodes, is also very informative.

● ●

Realization #5:
Risk Is Not a Synonym for Loss

The day came when the risk to remain a closed bud
became more painful than the risk to bloom.
— ANAÏS NIN

Ask any woman who is not taking financial responsibility what risk means, and it's likely she'll say "losing money." But the smart women I interviewed all said something very different. Take Pamela, the school-teacher-turned-entrepreneur. "I don't think you truly make money without taking some risks," she declared.

These women were neither blind to the chances they were taking nor indifferent to the downside possibilities. But they realized that *risk was not a four-letter word synonymous with loss,* nor was it a necessary evil or something to avoid. In fact, they considered risk essential to their future security. They understood one of the most fundamental laws of investing. Risk determines return. In other words, the profits we can generate on our investments are directly related to the amount of risk we are willing to take.

"I've never been afraid to take a risk," Pamela explained. "I just trust myself. I always have. I've always known that like a cat with nine lives, I would always end up on my feet." Very few women I interviewed, however, started out this brave and optimistic. For the majority, their willing-ness to take risks rarely came immediately or easily. It wasn't until they had arrived at all the other realizations we've discussed that they were ready to tackle this one.

I recall my interview with Phyllis, who had just been promoted to assis-tant vice president at a major brokerage firm. She was as comfortable in the stock market as Julia Child is in a kitchen. Dressed in a tailored navy suit, her short hair perfectly coifed, she looked the picture of a successful professional. Yet once, not so very long ago, she told me, she knew beans about money and couldn't care less. "I had no interest in money matters. I had married an MIT graduate and figured he had a secure future. I was a teacher and provided backup income, but basically I married someone who was going to provide financial security," she said. "When my husband would talk about stocks, I found the whole topic boring. I had no interest in investing, and I certainly had no interest in managing other people's money."

But the marriage ended. Suddenly Phyllis was a single mom. She had a two-year-old daughter, $10,000 in the bank, no alimony, and a rapidly dwindling cash reserve. Am I ever going to make it financially? she often wondered in panic. For a long time, she said, "I had this belief, as I was struggling, that someone would come in and life would get easier, finan-cially easier." But no one did. Finally she realized, "I had to accept the responsibility."

"How did you do it?" I asked her. Her response summed up what so many other women have told me. "*I had to take more risk.* I had to open myself up to things I was totally resistant to." She forced herself to learn about finances, even taking a job in insurance. "I hated the idea of selling life insurance, working solely on commission. But it was a way to learn. The more knowledge I had, the more involved I could get."

To her immense surprise, she "found it exciting to learn about invest-ments." Phyllis has done a good job investing for herself, and today she pulls in a six-figure salary managing other people's money.

"Aren't you ever afraid of the risks?" I inquired, hoping to disguise the fact that the question came from my own crippling fear. At the time I interviewed Phyllis, I was terrified of investing. Unable to forget my ex-husband's experiences, I associated the stock market, and its constant ups and downs, with surefire disaster. But like other smart women, Phyllis looked at these same ups and downs and saw a distinctly different scenario.

"I know that my investments will fluctuate," Phyllis said, shrugging. "I know my clients' will too. I just accept that. I am confident that over the long term I will do well. And so will my clients."

"Early on, even before I was with my present firm," she continued, "I learned the power of investing. I know stocks is the way to build wealth, far more than keeping money in a bank. People don't get rich in CDs."

I marveled at how Phyllis and so many others I was meeting had come to terms with risk. How they were willing to leave their comfort zones, face their fears, and take the heroic journey into the unknown, unpredictable realm of the investment world.

"I was very afraid of the stock market," another woman told me. "To me, it was a big crapshoot. The whole thing made no sense." But after having educated herself, she began to see it differently. "I still figure it's kind of a crapshoot. But you've got to be willing to take some risks in order to make a little extra. If you put in some time, do a little background work, you can eliminate the worst."

This realization that risk is not a synonym for loss is a crucial one for many women. Studies show that women are far more risk averse than men when it comes to investing. Not that being wary of risk is a bad thing. If wariness induces us to make premeditated, levelheaded, cautious decisions, then it works to our advantage. But disabling fear is a whole other story. Fear of risk keeps women out of the market, causes them to sell at the worst possible time or to buy the wrong investments. If fear of risk keeps women financially disadvantaged, then *understanding risk is what makes us wealthy*.

From my interviews, I saw that what gave smart women their courage was their understanding of three crucial things about risk.

1. They understood what risk really meant.
2. They learned how to stack the odds in their favor.
3. They figured out how much risk they could comfortably take.

1. Risk: What Is It?

Defining risk is a lot like describing a half glass of water. Is it half empty or half full? The *American Heritage Dictionary* defines risk as "possibility of suffering harm or loss." In other words, the glass is half empty. When you look at it in those terms, who in her right mind would willingly risk her hard-earned money? But the smart people I've spoken to had a very different viewpoint. Their glass is half full. When they look at the market, they see an opportunity for gain.

They realize that risk, by definition, does not mean gain or loss. Those are simply the possible outcomes. Risk in the market refers to volatility, and volatility refers to price swings. Look at any chart on the market or a particular security, and we'll see a big zigzag of ups and downs. The more a stock, or a market, moves up and down, the more risky it is.

But—here's the key—it's the overall direction, not the day-to-day bouncing, that matters. Take any twenty-year period, or ten years, for that matter, and a graph of the stock market will look like the upward slope of Mount Everest. Over time, the peaks go up ever higher and the lows don't dip quite as far down. The point is simply this: Volatility happens. It doesn't guarantee loss. It holds the possibility of big profits. Smart women realize this.

Fact Versus Fear: The Market Doesn't Matter

"We have a downturn in the real estate market now," a woman said, talking about her substantial holdings in real estate. Was she worried? I asked. Not really, she said. "All markets go up and all markets go down. This is one thing I learned about how money works. No market stays static. Stock markets, real estate markets, interest rate markets—they all go up and come down. They are always moving in one direction or the other." And these fluctuations? No big deal, she said. "They're just noise. Irritating noise."

If there is a trick to successful investing, it is this: Market fluctuations matter only when we cash in our assets, when we sell our holdings. If we need money in a few months or in the next year or two, then it pays to be conservative, putting our money where there is minimal upheaval. "Never buy stocks with money you'll need tomorrow," cautioned financial guru John Templeton. But the longer our time horizon, the less important those ups and downs are. If you've got, say, ten years, those fluctuations are irrelevant.

The market doesn't matter. Let those words be our mantra. Even the financial superstars adhere to this wisdom. "Ignore fluctuations," Templeton says. "Don't try to outguess the market. Buy quality and invest for the long term." Billionaire Warren Buffett calls the market direction "a coin flip. I invest in good businesses, managed by good people." And the legendary Peter Lynch acknowledges, "Whenever I go to a cocktail party, I can count on eight out of ten people to ask me how the market is. But I don't usually have an opinion. I just buy good stocks and stay invested."

Granted, for some people, this tactic takes a strong stomach. Trying to overlook market slumps while fully invested is like ignoring the steep drops on a roller coaster. And indeed, comparing the market to a roller coaster is so fitting it's become a cliché. But nowhere have I seen it better explained than in a Twentieth Century Mutual Funds newsletter. "Sure the ride is unsettling, but in reality, the real risk of injury is slim," observed the writer. "The thrill of the roller coaster comes only when the rider understands the difference between real and perceived risk."

Understanding the difference between real and perceived risk is the end result of this fifth realization.

The Real Risk

When I think about the difference between real and perceived risk, I am reminded of a line from *Alice in Wonderland*: "Nothing is as it seems. The skim milk masquerades as cream." This maxim could very well describe the stock market. When it comes to financial risk, nothing is as it seems. When our money is in a bank, it seems safe—after all, it's guaranteed by the federal government. Well, think again. What's safe in the short term is very risky over time. A savings account promising long-term security is like skim milk masquerading as cream.

"I was just talking to a client whose whole business account was in a bank," Phyllis, our brokerage house assistant vice president, told me. "I tried to explain to her how she was losing money. 'Look,' I said, 'your money is earning a little less than three percent. One third of that, roughly one percent, goes to taxes. Inflation will take another three percent. Figure it out. You're in the minus column. Years down the road, if you want to buy a car, you'll find your money hasn't kept pace with the increasing cost of that car.' "

We hear a lot of warnings about inflation. But such discussions are like admonitions on global warming. Despite its seriousness, the matter is easy to ignore because we can't actually see it, and by the time we feel its harmful effects, it's too late. Consider this graphic example from the College Board. Suppose you decide to set aside some money for your newborn baby's college education. You're taking no chances with that money, so you stuff $28,000—the average cost of four years of public college tuition—under a mattress. After all, even a bank could fall on hard times. Eighteen years later, you enroll your kid in college. Imagine your surprise when you find out what that roll of bills will buy you. If college costs continue to rise eight percent a year, you will have barely enough for one year. Even though you can't see it, like a hole in the ozone, the cost of everything will continue to grow.

Our real risk is not that the market may go down tomorrow. Our real risk is that our dollars won't buy what we need to buy when we are older or disabled. The riskiest financial investment decision we can make is deciding not to do anything or trying to stay "safe" with guaranteed returns.

There is only one way to shelter ourselves against "real risk" and genuinely safeguard our future, and that is by creating wealth through long-term asset building—investing our money in assets that will grow.

The Perceived Risk

Let's digress for a quick lesson in basic finance. There are only two ways to invest:

- as an owner
- as a lender

When we buy a stock, we own shares in the company. When we buy a bond, we lend money to the issuer of the bond. For the most part, stocks give us growth, bonds give us income. Stocks can make us more money. But stocks also have more volatility. As sure as a stock will go up, it will also go down.

Bonds, on the other hand, won't fluctuate nearly as much. And if we buy good ones, we're reasonably assured of getting back our original investment. So even though they don't provide as much growth, bonds or cash equivalents (CDs, treasury bills, money market funds) won't have those huge price swings. Therefore, many people assume that bonds and cash are less risky. In a Tower Perrins survey of employees' 401(k) plans, 32 percent of the respondents felt there was no risk in bonds. Fifty percent said that the guaranteed return was far more important than the potential for high return. The study's disturbing conclusion: People do not understand risk. Thus, the researchers explained, "Employees will ultimately fail to accumulate funds they need for retirement." (What's particularly distressing is that the same survey revealed that 75 percent of those polled are confident they *will* retire comfortably.)

I once clipped a financial advice column from a local newspaper. The reader's question: "I am young (29), single, and afraid of the stock market. What should I do with my $6000 bonus and the extra money from my paycheck?" The expert's answer: "Anyone who has a time horizon longer than seven years should have a large percentage of assets in stock." (The reader could just as well have been married and much older—sixty, even seventy. The columnist's response should be identical.)

The fear of stocks, the columnist explained, is the fear of "seeing your money go to zero. Facts support the opposite. Money left *out* of the stock market has a far greater chance of fading to zero by inflation."

Sure, stocks will go up and down a lot more than bonds or cash, but they will make you a heck of a lot more money. Since 1926, stocks have risen an average of 10 percent a year. Bonds, however, have returned 5.2 percent a year and treasuries 3.1 percent a year. Inflation, meanwhile, has averaged around 3 percent. That means stocks have earned more than seven percentage points above inflation, while bonds have offered only around 2 points.

As Peter Lynch points out in *Beating the Street*, "If you hope to have more money tomorrow than you have today, you've got to put a chunk of your assets into stock. . . . Sooner or later, a portfolio of stocks or mutual funds will turn out to be a lot more valuable than a portfolio of bonds or CDs or money market funds."

Smart women have come to realize this. "The market is a risk," Molly, a novice, yet a knowledgeable investor, told me during our interview. "But it's one of the better risks in town. Where else do people put their money? Banks? Why earn a passbook rate when you can do so much better in stocks or mutual funds?"

2. Stacking the Odds in Our Favor

As with *all* risks—whether crossing the street, traveling by plane, or buying a stock—there are certain events over which we have no control. The economy can go to pot, a company can hit the skids, the market can turn scary. In fact, it's almost guaranteed we'll experience at least one of these occurrences, probably our first time out. While we can't prevent such things from happening, there are steps we can take to soften the blow and protect ourselves from harm. A woman named Judy once told me, "The whole idea is to minimize risk by taking out the jagged line."

There are three approaches we can take to help neutralize the jagged line:

- Think long-term.
- Structure before stock picking.
- Invest with discipline.

Think long-term

"If you try to get rich quick, you may get poor even quicker," Esther Berger writes in *Money Smart*. And financial columnist Andrew Tobias warns, "The worst thing you can do with $3000 is to try to turn it into $10,000 real fast. You will lose it."

Going for quick profits is truly risky, in the most derogatory sense. Trying to time the market has the same odds as a game of blackjack. It's a virtual gamble. Timing means jumping in and out of the market, hoping to avoid the lows and get in at the highs. Timing rarely works, for the simple reason we noted earlier—no one knows how the market will do. There is no way we can be sure precisely which day will be the best and which day the worst. Better to leave our money alone than try to second-guess.

Take this example: If you were in the market every day from 1980 to 1989, you would have earned 17.5 percent on your money, but if you missed the thirty best days, your earnings would have been only 6.5 percent. Or try this: If you had put one dollar in the market in 1979, by 1995 you'd have $54. But if you were out of the market during the ten best months of those sixteen years, your dollar would be worth only $2.75 today.

Speculating is a gamble that rarely pays off. Moreover, trading in and out of the market is expensive. Even if we get lucky, a big hunk of our winnings will go to pay capital gains taxes. There's more truth than humor in the old saw "Investors drive Cadillacs, traders drive Chevrolets."

Phyllis spoke to me at length about this point. "I think people get really hurt when they tamper with their investments," she explained. "People who move their money around too much usually sell at the wrong time." She recalled a recent example. "I just talked to someone the other day who had $2,500 in stock that he forgot he had, and it's now worth $35,000."

"You're in for the long haul," Phyllis tells her clients. "Up-and-down fluctuations don't mean anything. The only day that matters is the day you're going to sell." Still, she admitted, "Some days I get squeamish, but I don't let it run my decisions."

Virtually every woman mentioned the wisdom of this long-term approach, many of them having learned their lesson the hard way. Lucy, for example, worked with a broker who did a lot of buying and selling. "One day, he called me about another investment, and I just couldn't handle the financial wheeling and dealing any longer," she said. "I put the account on hold. The way he talked, we were making money and everything was great. But by my math, when I added in brokerage fees, we lost money." She found another broker. "He's a buy-and-hold type," she told me. "I really like working with him."

Naomi, who once traded heavily with a broker, told me the same thing.

"It costs a lot of money to trade, and you don't get any real value. By the time you're finished, with trading fees and taxes, the gain is so small. It was a good lesson. I buy for the long term now."

So what do we do when the market starts heading south? Smart people stay put. "Everything I read told me that if I was diversified and could sit through the ups and downs, I'd end up okay," a woman in her late forties explained. "Most of our stuff is for retirement in about twenty years. I rode out the crash in 1987, and I stayed in during all the corrections we've had. And I have done very well."

Selling when the market is at its lowest, then buying when it's at its highest, is the worst thing we can do. Louis Rukeyser, host of *Wall Street Week*, once said the foolproof way to lose money in the stock market was to "buy when stocks are hurtling in the stratosphere and everybody tells you it's the easiest game in town. Then sell them the first time the market trips and tumbles and everybody tells you that the game is over from here on in and only an idiot would be crazy enough to hold stocks."

Surprisingly, at least to me at the time, many of the women I interviewed told me that when the market crashed in 1987, instead of panicking, they rushed out and picked up more stock at bargain prices. How did they have the nerve to do that? I asked, recalling that I sold everything in a fit of sheer terror. I'll never forget one woman's answer: "History was on my side," she told me. "I know the stock market always comes back."

The women who, like myself, had done otherwise learned from this mistake. One woman I spoke to had just invested $10,000 when the whole market tumbled (in what is known as a "correction") and took her stocks down with it. "I pulled out," she told me. But since then, she said, "I've learned the system knows better than I do. It does work. The truth is, if you are out at the wrong time, you can miss the whole deal. If you were out January and February last year, you didn't get any gains for the year. You have to commit to trusting the system. It works better than going in and out when panic strikes. That much I have learned. It works better to go with the system than to be emotional."

The best way to protect ourselves against the market swings is to have a long time horizon—five to ten years. One or two bad years makes little difference over time. "If you think of risk as the chance you'll lose money in the short term, then stocks are indeed extremely risky," declared a reporter in the *Wall Street Journal*. "But if you have the tenacity to stick with your stock investment over five years or longer, then the chance of losing money is slim." In fact experts tell us that the probability of losing money in a diversified, well-managed portfolio of stocks over 20 years is practically zero.

- Based on the Standard & Poor's 500 Index, since 1926, the chances of losing money over one year is 29 percent; over five years, 11 percent; over ten years, 3 percent; over twenty years, 0 percent.
- Even if we bought in August 25, 1987, at the very top, before the market crashed and didn't return to record heights until July 1991, we'd still be ahead by 57 percent as of 1995, with an average gain of 6 percent annually.

There will always be the Chicken Littles who swear the sky is falling. It's very tempting to follow them to the nearest exit. I was very tempted to bail out in 1994, a very bad year for most investors, me included. My portfolio lost money, and 1995 was predicted to be just as bad. But it was kind of like being in a rocky relationship with a good man. I felt good about the choices I had made, so I stuck it out. Imagine my smugness when I read in the *International Herald Tribune* at the end of 1995, "Investors who listened to the majority of Wall Street pundits at the beginning of 1995 would have stayed out of the market—and missed out on the best returns in about 20 years." My stock portfolio was up over 30 percent, clearly offsetting my 6 percent loss the year before.

I learned from the smart women to ignore not only the daily dips but also the negative news stories. A fascinating study conducted with graduate business students at the Massachusetts Institute of Technology proved the value of this tactic. Half the students received frequent stock updates, the others got no news at all. Those who received no information were far more successful investors. As Louis Rukeyser commented in his financial newsletter, "Over time, indifference to the market will make you an impressive amount of money."

Phyllis agreed. In managing her own money, she told me, "I want to be sure it's well allocated, and then, unless something is drastically wrong with a particular fund, I just leave it there."

• Structure a Portfolio Before Picking Stocks

Phyllis referred to a crucial tool used for flattening out the jagged line in our investments: *asset allocation.* In the previous chapter, we spoke of the importance of diversification in structuring a portfolio, of not putting all our eggs in one basket or one company. Asset allocation is the term used to describe *how* we divide, or diversify, our money among different markets, or asset classes, and types of securities. Many people will spend hours sweating over which stock to buy, but the real trick to making money in the market is not whether we pick IBM or Microsoft. It's how we split the total pie. The way a portfolio is structured, not the particular stocks themselves, determines a portfolio's performance.

Remember we said there are only five places, or asset classes, where we can invest? What we must ask ourselves, before anything else, is: How do we divide our investment cash among these five classes? In other words, how much will we put in stocks? In bonds? In cash? And, for some, in real estate and commodities? Each of these asset classes can be further divided into subclasses. How much will we put into small-company stocks? Large-company stocks? Foreign stocks? Foreign bonds? Corporate bonds? Government bonds? Figuring out how to divide our assets among these categories is the most critical investment decision we will make. This one decision accounts for 93 percent of our performance. (According to research, only 2 percent of our return comes from stock picking, another 2 percent from timing, and 3 percent from luck.)

"The risk of each holding is far less than the riskiness of the entire portfolio," my favorite columnist, Jonathan Clements, explained in the *Wall Street Journal.* "High-risk investments can be tamed when combined with other holdings." Why? "Investments don't all move in lockstep."

He gives this example: "U.S. securities got roughed up in 1987 and 1994, but foreign stocks, specifically Japan, provided offsetting gains.

Tables were turned in 1992, when U.S. stocks came to the rescue as foreign shares tumbled."

The message is clear: Don't get hung up on the riskiness of a specific security. And don't try to predict the market. If we put together a widely diversified portfolio of well-managed funds or good solid companies and top-rated bonds, over time we should do well.

How do we decide which way to allocate our money? This depends mostly on our age and ability to earn money outside our investments. Remember, the more time we can hold our investments, the less our risk of loss. Typically, an older woman with no means of support outside her social security checks would want a reliable portfolio, mostly bonds and dividend-paying stocks in quality companies that provide sufficient income with little fluctuation. But a younger career woman would be better off with the majority of her holdings in stocks. Problem is, studies show that women of all ages tend to shy away from stocks. The Oppenheimer study reported that women keep an average of 14 percent of their portfolio in equities, compared to 31 percent for men. This was not the case with the smart women I spoke to.

One of the oldest women I interviewed was a widow in her mid-seventies, a retired psychologist. Though she had a substantial amount of her money in treasury notes and municipal bonds for income and guaranteed return, she had about 40 percent in individual stocks, which she actively managed. "I read the *Wall Street Journal* every day," she told me proudly, "and I watch the market like a hawk. I may be older, but I plan on living a lot longer, and I want to make sure I have enough money." Besides, she added, laughing, "I have expensive tastes."

The youngest woman I talked to was a twenty-six-year-old bank analyst, who had 90 percent of her investments in stocks and the rest in cash. "I think I have way too much cash," she confided. "If I were a more astute investor, I'd have 95 percent in equities and 5 percent in cash. What do I want with idle cash just sitting around? If I weren't working, I'd feel differently. But I am working. My husband's working. I want to get as much growth as possible. I don't need income-producing securities like bonds, which would give me more income but increase my taxes."

A woman in her mid-thirties, who lived off the income from her portfolio, told me, "I have almost half my holdings in real estate, which gives me income. A fourth is in stock funds for growth. A little less than a fourth is in bonds for additional income. The rest is in savings for emergency."

Many of the women I interviewed had several portfolios, with different allocations for different goals: children's education, retirement, buying a home, or income to live off of. Several even had a "fun fund," earmarked for trips, fancy dinners, and various luxuries. Each portfolio had a somewhat different mix of stocks, bonds, and cash. How did they figure out how to do this? Some did it on their own. Most of them, however, sat down with a professional advisor, preferably a financial planner. (More about planners, and other professionals, in the following chapter.)

"Stockbrokers never talked to me about allocation of funds," Frances told me. "A financial planner was the first to sit down with these pie charts. How come brokers never asked me about the big picture?"

Once she saw the big picture, she said, "investing was not as frightening to me. Over the last year, I have made a lot of changes, into more aggressive funds. I've learned to think of things in cycles or longer terms. Nobody really explained to me about cycles in the market, or staying in for the long term, riding things out." It makes a big difference in our emotional well-being and our capacity to accept risk when we look at the total picture and draw up a blueprint for taking action.

"Coming to peace with money in our life is something that eludes most people," financial advisor Ann Lieberman told me. "I look for lessons among my clients about people who are at peace with money. Part of being at peace with money is coming in here and asking me to lay out a plan for them, so they know what they want to do. Whether it's to get their kids through college or retire comfortably or buy a second home, when people have their goals straight, when they can set priorities and make choices, they are at peace."

I am reminded of one woman who struck me as especially calm and confident with money. I asked her secret. She answered, "I've taken my time, and I am very cautious. My money is well divided between stocks, bonds, and my house. Every month I withdraw $400 from my savings and invest it. Anytime I discover extra money, I write a check."

This woman not only had a plan; she had the discipline to stick to it. This kind of discipline is critical to successful investing.

• *Invest with Discipline*

The majority of women I interviewed adhered to a system of periodic investing or, as it is known in market lingo, *dollar cost averaging*. We mentioned this approach in the last chapter when we discussed the importance of starting small and going slow. Dollar cost averaging means investing whatever we can afford, whether it's $25, $250, or $2,500, at a regular time—every month, every quarter—no matter what the market is doing.

By investing regularly, we avoid investing at the top of the market or at the bottom. And if the market drops or it's at a low, we'll be accumulating more shares at a better price. If we set up a plan—with our bank, brokerage firm, or mutual fund company—to shift the money automatically from our paycheck to our investment account, we eliminate the possibility of procrastination, resistance, or spending the money we meant to invest. Automatic investing makes discipline a whole lot easier. Even the most savvy women admitted that.

"Very early on, I made the decision that I had to isolate money on a systematic basis, doing automatic investing," Phyllis, a stockbroker, told me. "What happened was that I'd bring in the money and spend it. I have to isolate it or it goes. You have to create a system. My secretary wanted to buy a house. So she systematically saved money for a down payment, and she bought it. It takes discipline."

3. How Much Risk Can I Tolerate?

All this talk about risk sounds so, well, benign. And the formulas for investing make it seem pretty easy. Why, then, do so many of us quiver at the mere thought of investing in equities? For this one simple reason: We're talking about our money, our basic source of safety and well-being, our very survival. It's a rare individual who doesn't get spooked when the market goes sour—no matter what the reality for loss actually is. It's like watching a horror movie. We know it's not real, but we're still gripping the edge of our seats during the scary parts. And when our money is at stake, some of us can brave the scary parts a lot better than others.

I found no correlation between a woman's financial intelligence and her risk tolerance. Some of the women I interviewed relished the idea of such risky investments as small-company stocks, emerging-market funds, second mortgages, even venture capital. Others were self-proclaimed chickens. Most were somewhere in between. What I did find among smart women was that they eventually figured out how much risk they could comfortably take and then stayed within those parameters. "I am not the shrewdest investor," one woman admitted. "I have a lot of money in cash, probably too much. The rest is in fairly conservative funds. I may get more aggressive someday. But I have to know I can sleep at night."

In terms of assessing our own attitude to risk, the question we should ask ourselves is not: Should I take a risk and invest in the market? The answer to that is an emphatic yes. The critical question is this: *How much risk can I take?* The answer: enough to stay ahead of inflation but still sleep at night.

"I try to put my money in instruments where I can sleep at night," Marion told me. "I call it the 'sleep continuum' from one to ten. Ten is things like second mortgages with people who have unlisted phone numbers, and one is a savings account. Then I look at all the variables of the investment and paint the worst-case scenario and put it through the sleep-at-night test."

The degree of risk we can take and still get a good night's sleep will be different for each of us. There are all kinds of quizzes in all sorts of publications that are supposed to reveal our risk tolerance. But in real life, risk is like spicy food. We have to taste it to know how much we can stand. We'll never really know our risk tolerance—that is, how much volatility we can stomach—until we actually have our money in the market.

Phyllis agrees. "You can read lots of books. But once you start investing, you really learn what risk is all about. You can read what a growth and income fund is, and they tell you it's not a risky investment, but when you experience a fall of fifteen percent, you see what risk really is."

Some women tried their hand at risky stuff and found out it wasn't for them. "I saw my father doing all these high-risk options. I decided to play too," a woman in her forties told me. "Within a few months I was in way over my head and realizing I'm not that kind of risk taker. I wasn't sleeping at night. My daughter finally said, 'Mom, get a life. I don't think the market agrees with you.'"

Others thrive on big risks. "The risky stuff is what keeps me involved," an older woman told me. "If I didn't have that piece, it would be boring, boring, boring. I could make my portfolio simpler, less volatile, but I chose not to because it's just more fun this way." Still, she conceded, "I've been very careful and conservative with most of my money, risking only what I could afford to lose."

Still others were willing to take moderate risks, not because they delighted in the excitement, but because they simply weren't afraid of loss. For example, Linda Pei had fled from China with her family, leaving all their belongings behind. "Because I started out with zero," she said, "I probably can take more risk than my husband. If you've once had nothing, and know what it is like, you know you can survive. You're not as scared. If I lose everything, I know I can start over. My feeling is I can always make it."

Many others were just the opposite. "I realize I am a very conservative investor," Renee told me. "When I just think about taking risks, I get a physical sensation. My stomach turns over. My heart beats faster. My breathing turns shallow. I don't want to live like that. I know slow and steady gets people in good shape as much as huge risks. I don't like big risks. I know that about me."

Testing Our Tolerance: Climbing the Investment Pyramid

Whether our stomach turns somersaults just thinking about risk, or we're stimulated by the action, the *investment pyramid* is an important concept to understand when we begin to invest. It's the principal method for easing into potentially risky waters while protecting ourselves from going under. Imagine a pyramid containing four levels of investments, where the least risky investment occupies the bottom stratum and each level gets progressively riskier. The higher the climb, the greater the volatility.

We invest by going *up* the pyramid, starting at the bottom level, which consists of cash or cash equivalents—CDs, treasuries, a decent emergency reserve. This is our sleep-at-night money. There is no risk here

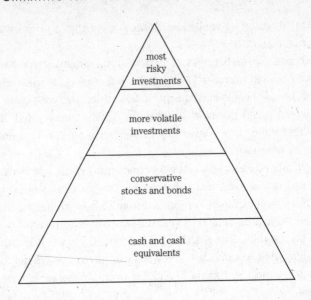

except inflation and taxes. We have certainty at this level of getting our original investment back. If we need money immediately, this is where we go. We should have enough cash set aside for periods of unemployment, unforeseen emergencies, or unexpected expenses.

When we have sufficient cash savings, we move up to level two, stocks and bonds. This is our inflation-fighting money. These are liquid assets that can be turned into cash fairly quickly. But because they fluctuate more than, say, treasuries, if we have to cash them in when the market is down, we'll be selling at a loss. The money that's invested here, therefore, is for a longer time frame.

The third level consists of more volatile stocks, like emerging markets, foreign funds, and junk bonds. Here the fluctuations are bigger than at level two, but the gains can be greater. These investments may be "wild and crazy," according to the *Wall Street Journal*, but they sure can ratchet up returns.

Finally, at the tip of the pyramid are the wildest investments of all: limited partnerships, venture capital, commodities, derivatives. The gains here can be colossal, but the downside can be too. These are the kinds of investments that have made people fortunes or forced them into bankruptcy. Many people choose never to climb to the top. And without question, no one should ever start out here.

Remember, we always begin by working our way *up* the pyramid. Why? As someone once explained it to me, imagine the pyramid turned upside down, balancing on its tip. Not very secure. Imagine investing there first. You'd have a very shaky, insecure portfolio that could topple with a feather.

"I watched my brother lose all his inheritance in a bad real estate investment," one woman told me. "I learned you don't put all your eggs in one basket. I learned you start with a safe base of cash. Then you move into conservative investments. Then you go into more aggressive things." Another woman learned the hard way. "I think I made a big mistake getting into limited partnerships first thing," she told me. "If I had to do it all over again, I would put a much smaller amount in and start much more conservatively."

How much we put in each level depends on our personal goals, our risk tolerance, and our age. But Phyllis suggests two rules of thumb:

- In terms of the first level, "Three months living expenses is good, six months if someone doesn't have job security."
- When we move into the second level, "the best thing we can do is get tax-deferred growth on our money. Any person who is eligible for a 401(k) should put the maximum in before doing any personal investing."

The Many Rewards of Risk

> *"Sure you can fly, but that cocoon's got to go."*
> —ANONYMOUS

The willingness to trust ourselves to take a risk, whatever that means to us, is what investing is all about. If we start at the bottom of the investment pyramid, allocate our investments properly, and give them five or so years to grow, then we're in good stead. Remember, even a conservative portfolio will make more money over time than cash sitting in a bank.

"You don't have to have dazzling results to do extremely well," writes Jeremy Segal, author of *Stocks for the Long Run*. "Even average stock market returns will, with time, dramatically beat bonds, money markets, and treasury bills."

If our investments go up, we can pat ourselves on the back. And if they go down, we should still sleep well at night, knowing that time is on our side. Eventually we'll awake to discover that not only are we wealthier, but we've grown personally.

I once read some words, by a woman named Laura Davis, about the real reward of taking risk. I cut out the quote and saved it for moments when my self-assurance wears thin: "Through the experience I have had and the risks I have taken, I have gained courage and confidence. I didn't start with the courage and confidence. I started with the risk."

Still, staring risk in the face can feel like we're poised on the edge of a steep cliff, looking straight down into a perilous drop. To those whose fear of heights is greater than their urge to fly, the idea of jumping will seem unthinkable. If such is your case, the next realization should feel particularly welcome.

••• CHAPTER SEVEN RECAPPED •••

Realization—Investing entails risk. But risk is *not* another word for loss. In truth, the worst financial risk we can take is doing nothing. Money sitting in a bank loses its purchasing power. Money wisely invested increases our future security. Sure the market will fluctuate, but we can protect ourselves from short-term loss with a long-term horizon and a properly allocated portfolio.

To Do

1. Figure out what is the best allocation plan for your age and lifestyle needs. You can pick up a free booklet at Charles Schwab, "Investing Made Easy," which explains (in simple language and colorful graphics) various allocation plans. (It sure helped me. So did their free lunchtime seminars.) Most mutual fund families, like Fidelity, Vanguard, or T. Rowe Price, have

similar booklets available. You need only call and request one. (You'll often see them advertised in financial publications.)

2. If you are currently invested, check that your portfolio is appropriately allocated. On paper, put your holdings into categories: stocks or stock funds, bonds or bond funds, cash, real estate, and any commodities. Then, to make sure each category is properly diversified, divide each of these categories into subcategories. Stocks, for example, can be divided according to size, country, and industry. (You would not want all your stocks to be in, say, the computer industry.) Bonds include municipal, corporate, and savings bonds.

If you've never invested, you may want to wait until you read the next chapter to take action.

3. Join the American Association of Individual Investors (625 N. Michigan Ave., Chicago, IL 60611), and the National Center for Women and Retirement Research (Long Island University, Southampton, NY 11968). Read their publications.

4. Join an investment club. It's a great way to get started. Members make small monthly contributions, which are pooled to purchase a diversified portfolio of stocks. Once you understand the fundamentals, you can apply them to your own investments. Contact the National Association of Investors Corporation (NAIC; P.O. Box 220, Royal Oak, MI 48068) for information.

Meanwhile, here are the NAIC's four principles of investing, as good advice as any you'll ever see:

1. Invest a set sum once a month, regardless of market conditions.
2. Reinvest dividends and capital gains immediately.
3. Buy growth stocks—companies that are increasing at a rate faster than industry in general and should continue to do.
4. Diversify. Invest in different fields.

Chapter Eight

● ●

Realization #6:
I Don't Have to Do This Alone

*Our chief want in life is somebody who shall
make us do what we can.*
—EMERSON

As my interviews progressed, a paradox emerged. At the same time these women spoke of their self-reliance—how they had forsworn a prince and taken full charge of their finances—they talked frequently of their reliance on others. It was as if the same women who realized "no one is going to do this for me" simultaneously came to another realization: *"I don't have to do this alone."* This proved to be vital. Women who are smart with money don't get that way in isolation.

You may have noticed this realization showing up in the stories told throughout the book. Indeed, every woman I talked to told me that she had sought help as a way of getting started, that she reached out when she got stuck, and that she continued seeking counsel on a regular basis. Almost everyone requested advice and referrals from friends and family members. Many accepted guidance from mentors and advisors. Most worked closely with stockbrokers or portfolio managers. Some even put together teams made up of, say, an accountant, a lawyer, and a financial planner.

Face it. There's an awful lot to know about money management. We can have a heck of a time trying to figure out what to do on our own. Most of us simply don't have the time, temperament, or desire, not to mention the training, to manage our money all by ourselves. But there are plenty of people who do. There are people who spend their professional lives doing nothing but studying finances—stockbrokers, financial planners, portfolio managers, insurance agents, real estate brokers, estate planners, accountants, lawyers, and bankers. These professionals, each with a special area of expertise, provide invaluable advice and time-saving services, and they can help us avoid costly mistakes.

But it's not just financial professionals who can be helpful. Peer support is virtually indispensable, especially for women. Linking up with other people is an essential part of our nature. Boys, by and large, have been brought up to be tough, independent, and self-reliant. Autonomy comes naturally to them. Girls tend to be relation oriented. Numerous surveys have found that while men define success in terms of money earned, women point to family and personal relationships as measures of success. Perhaps it's the way we were raised or the result of our genetic predisposition as childbearers. Whatever the reason, we tend to thrive on the synergy of mutual support.

Supportive relationships are like vitamins for our soul, fortifying our will to succeed, boosting our ability to take action. One woman told me that her husband has become her financial mentor. "He prods me—Go for it!—all the time." Simple words of support and encouragement like these can turn our financial journey from a frustrating, arduous, and fearful experience to one that inspires and empowers.

"When we come out of isolation, exchange ideas, information, experiences, we also create solutions for each other," philanthropist Tracy Gary, who inherited her wealth, once told me. "This collective experience transforms us. We no longer feel money is a burden, but money becomes a tool for changing our lives."

When in her twenties, Tracy served on a board of a nonprofit foundation. During meetings, she began to notice that whenever money was discussed in a mixed group, the men always dominated the discussion and, astonishingly, the women always let them. And she was doing the same thing. Tracy, who prided herself on being outspoken, was as silent as the rest when the topic turned to money and men were around.

"I was unconsciously triggered back into some kind of old family dynamic where the men knew about business, the men were in charge," she told me. She began to see that women's silence was a critical hurdle they had to overcome. She expressed her frustration to a friend, and together they came up with the idea for a retreat, a day for sharing their feelings and telling their stories about money. For most of the women who attended, it was the first time they had talked so openly about money.

"It was a magical experience for me," Tracy recalls. "It was powerful to have these people willing to say what they felt and to know I wasn't the only one who felt that way."

Out of that experience, Tracy got the idea for Managing Inherited Wealth (MIW), a financial support group for women who had inherited money. MIW was meant to be a kind of safe harbor where women could talk openly about money and learn from each other. Today MIW, now part of Resourceful Women, has received nationwide media attention, and thousands of women have attended its meetings. When I first learned of MIW's existence, however, it was still a small, fledgling organization.

I heard about MIW right around the time the ATM machine refused to give me money. I went to a meeting partly out of curiosity, mostly out of desperation. It was one of the best things I ever did for myself. There were maybe ten women attending, all ages, casually dressed, sitting in a circle in one of the women's living rooms. Tracy was among them, and she spoke first. She explained that this was a time to say whatever we wanted. We could share our feelings about money, discuss any problems we were having with it, boast of any strides we had made, and ask for whatever help we might need. Everything we said would be held in the strictest confidence.

My heart began pounding. I had never discussed my money situation with anyone—not with my therapist, whom I had been seeing weekly for two years; not with my best friends, who would never have understood how having money could be a problem; and not even with my family, except for occasional attempts that went nowhere. Now I was supposed to open up to a bunch of total strangers. But listening to each woman candidly express her fears, confusion, insecurity—the same demons I had been wrestling with—gave me the courage to speak up.

I told my story, all of it. I confessed that my husband had been losing money and I didn't know what to do. No one looked at me as if I were a hopeless dummy. Instead they gave me ideas. Everyone thought I should talk to a financial advisor. They shared their own experiences with finding one. And they suggested several names to contact. It had never occurred to me, until that meeting, to seek help from an advisor. In fact, I'm not sure I even knew such people existed.

That one meeting gave me a place to start and the courage to act. It was from these women's referrals that I found Bob Lovett, the money manager who gave me my first real lesson in understanding money. Beyond that, it broke the shame of secrecy and the isolation of silence I had been living with for years.

The Legacy of Secrecy and Silence

Secrecy and isolation are frequent companions to most women on their journey to financial independence. Why do so many of us struggle in a vacuum? Why don't more of us reach out for help?

Lauren was an energetic entrepreneur who nervously nibbled popcorn the whole time we talked. She had recently acquired another company, which dramatically increased her net profits. When I asked her what had been her greatest challenge financially, she needed no time to consider her response. "I had no one to talk to," she answered. "That was the one thing I found most difficult. Women do not talk about money. They just don't. It's like a secret, this big secret."

In our culture, money *is* a big secret. Society treats the subject as if it's off-limits. "Money is hardly spoken of in parlors without apology," Emerson observed over a century ago. Little has changed. Money is still shrouded in secrecy and silence. "I always felt it was unmentionable," another woman told me, explaining why she had so much difficulty talking to anybody about money. "I felt it had to be hidden, like it was crass."

Freud likened our secretive nature around money to sex. "Money questions will be treated by cultured people in the same manner as sexual matters; with the same inconsistency, prudishness, and hypocrisy," he said. These days, however, we're far more apt to talk about sex than money.

Washington-based psychotherapist and author Olivia Mellan agrees. "Over the last decade, talk about sex has come out in the open," she notes, "but talk about money is just beginning to come out. It's easier for my clients to approach childhood trauma and sexual problems than to talk about money and what it represents."

Interestingly, it's not just their clients who have a hard time talking about money. Three major surveys of psychotherapists revealed that money matters were the most difficult subject for the therapists themselves to discuss with their patients. In fact, when the American Psychological Association sent out a survey on the subject to its members, few bothered to send it back. The money survey had the lowest rate of return among all their sponsored polls. "Either therapists believe money is not a worthwhile research variable," concluded one APA official, "or money is part of the new obscenity in which we talk more freely about sex but never mention money."

"I get so frustrated," a young woman complained. "You see someone who is really good with money, but you can't just say, 'What are you doing with it?' We're raised not to talk about it." Indeed, most of us were brought up with this attitude. How many of us talked freely about money with our parents? A *USA Today* poll reveals that 62 percent of respondents never discussed money with their children. No surprise, the parents' hushed attitude creates a legacy of discomfort for the children.

"The taboo against speaking about money in our families is usually so strong that to ask about it is to seem rude, or worse, greedy," Norma Gallagher wrote in the *Family Therapy Networker*. "We collude in keeping money's role in our lives secret and its power over us intact."

While money is rarely dinner-table discussion in most families, the problem is even more insidious for women. Traditionally, parents are far more likely to give financial information to their sons than their daughters. In our society, there is still the belief that "nice girls" don't talk about money. Over and over again, women told me that they were brought up differently than their male siblings. "My father sat down and told my brothers everything about his financial situation," one woman recalled.

"When I asked him how much money he had, he said, 'That's not something you need to know about.' "

If we can't talk about money with our family, we certainly won't discuss our financial issues with friends. It doesn't matter if we're rich or poor. Either way, we are hush-hush about our finances. We're afraid others will judge us for not having enough. Or we're afraid others will resent, criticize, or envy our affluence. "We live in a culture that venerates money and also thinks people who have it are disgusting," a psychologist once told me.

"Money is my big secret," admitted a young heiress, who has never even told her therapy group she is wealthy. "I'm afraid if people know I'm rich, they'll write me off without getting to know me first." When her friend unexpectedly dropped by her home one day and for the first time saw her expensive furnishings, this young heiress felt so uncomfortable she blurted out, "Are you still going to be my friend?"

Many times we feel stupid and vulnerable, and then think we're the only ones who feel this way. A struggling thirty-four-year-old told me that it took her years to ask for financial guidance, because she was so ashamed of her ignorance. "I kept thinking that people would find out I didn't know what I was talking about, that I had never learned any solid financial skills," she admitted meekly.

This secrecy around money is not only frustrating. It's debilitating. It hampers the inner work and delays the outer work. Secrecy breeds fear. Fear creates paralysis. Paralysis intensifies fear. The cycle perpetuates itself. It's time we end the silence. As long as money is a mystery, something out there, something other people do but no one discusses, it feels out of bounds, untouchable, unknowable, unapproachable, and we're afraid of it.

Shattering the Silence

How do we end this silence and secrecy? By taking a bite of the forbidden fruit, so to speak, by reaching out and speaking candidly about money. We can start by talking to other women we know.

Numerous women I spoke to voiced immense relief at finding someone else with whom they could finally discuss money. "I've found some friends I can talk to," one woman told me. "You know, like: 'What are you doing? Who are you using? Are you scared?' It's made such a difference."

We can truly make a remarkable difference in one another's financial journey. Each of us has something we can teach, regardless of our level of knowledge. We can learn from each others' mistakes and draw inspiration from each others' successes. We can use each other as sounding boards, role models, and sources of encouragement.

Aside from individual conversations with friends, a number of the women I interviewed participated in some kind of support group, educational forum, or loosely formed financial consciousness raising. A number of women told me they were members of investment clubs. They would meet monthly, pool their money and research, and make investment decisions collectively. These clubs have gained enormous popularity among men and women as an enjoyable, social, hands-on way to learn about the ins and outs of the market.

Other women I talked to gathered informally. JoAnne, a computer programmer, met with a group of coworkers for a monthly luncheon to discuss, among other things, finances. JoAnne's salary was adequate, but she never gave it much thought. During one of these lunches, however, she recognized that she needed to become financially active. "These women told me I couldn't just leave my money in a bank, because inflation was going to eat it up," she said. "One woman had gone to the library and discovered a financial newsletter. She told me about it, and I got it. Then we all subscribed. And we all started following its suggestions."

As a result, JoAnne started putting anywhere from $50 to $300 a month in no-load mutual funds (funds without sales fees), and over the past few years she has accumulated a portfolio worth over $10,000. "My goal is to get money for my kids' college," she told me. "I have some time to do that, so I'm thinking about getting a little riskier. I've made an appointment with this guy I know, a financial consultant. I'll take one hour of his time and see what his ideas are."

Beyond peer support, the majority of women I interviewed, like JoAnne, turned to financial professionals. "The easiest way to get a grip on financial matters," declared a recent issue of *Business Week* magazine, "is to find an advisor you can trust."

These women used a variety of advisors for planning, investing, and other financial activities. Some hired people to directly manage their money. Others invested in professionally managed mutual funds. Still others invested independently with a stockbroker. Nearly all, at some point, conferred with a financial planner. There is a plethora of specialists in the field. In the past, these categories of advisors were sharply defined. Today their services often overlap. The question is, where do we start?

Start with a Plan

When I put that question to women I interviewed—Where is the best place to start when we're ready to invest?—the overwhelming majority recommended a financial planner, someone who will help us step back, see the big picture, analyze our financial situation, and prepare a program to meet our specific needs and objectives.

I remember when my friend Lisa was trying to put some money aside but was having a hard time getting started. "No matter how hard I work, I can't seem to make any headway," she told me forlornly. "I wanted my husband to handle the finances, but he could care less about money. The message is obvious. I've got to figure it out all by myself."

"Not quite," I said. "You're right, it's up to you, no one will do it for you. But you don't have to do everything all by yourself." I urged her to make an appointment with a financial planner, someone who would sit down, ask her the right questions, get her to focus, and help her set goals.

"But I've been a fool all these years. How do I explain that?" she pleaded. "I don't even know the first thing to ask."

"It doesn't matter," I promised. "That's their job. Good advisors will draw out all the information they need by asking the right questions. If we don't know what our objectives are, part of their job is helping us figure them out." And I told her what other financial planners had told me.

"No advisor I know will expect you to be knowledgeable," Ann Lieberman had said. "Where would you learn? They don't teach it in school. It's an interactive process. Strategies develop in the dialogue between the provider and the user, just like when you go to a doctor, lawyer, or accountant."

Ann described how the process works. "My first question to people is usually, 'What's wrong?' People don't come to me unless something hurts, something isn't working. I keep asking them, 'Anything else?' I try to uncover all the problems," she explains. "If someone is embarrassed about feeling stupid, I say that learning theories claim it takes seven exposures to new information to get it. You have six more to go."

Then, she said, she may suggest doing a financial plan or, depending on the situation, she may refer the person to someone else, like an accountant or a lawyer. "If we do a plan," she said, "I give them a checklist of what to bring: wills, any partnership or prenuptial agreements, back tax returns, insurance, investments, employee benefit manuals, things like that."

Another financial planner, Elliot Chernin, asks for two things: "their most recent tax return and a balance sheet of what they own and what they owe." But, he quickly added, "People really don't need to bring me any more than the one thing they have on their mind related to financial matters. Should I buy a home? Am I putting away enough for retirement? What will happen to my estate after I die? Can you help me make sense of my finances? Am I saving enough? Things amplify from that."

He described what he tries to do for his clients. "I want to make sure people have the insurance safety they need and some cash reserves to help them over the bad spots, then start a systematic investment program, no matter how small. In the beginning, it's getting into the habit. And," he emphasized, "I want to make sure they eliminate expensive non-sensical debt like credit cards, because no one gets ahead paying fifteen percent."

There are several benefits to financial planning besides developing an overall plan. For one thing, working with a good financial planner takes the pressure off. We don't have to learn everything on our own. "A financial planner is like a personal trainer," Ann Lieberman said. "If you are going to achieve excellence, you must have a coach." And for women, who are relationship oriented, it's natural to learn with someone's help.

Plus, when we feel stuck, it sure helps when someone is there to get us started, and having another person hold us accountable is a good way to stay on track. (This is the premise behind the success of Weight Watchers.) As Elliot told me, "I become a nag to make sure my clients do what they should be doing."

The key here, as I told Lisa, is to find someone you feel comfortable with, who is willing to teach you, and who charges a reasonable fee for his or her services (as opposed to a commission). This would most likely be a financial planner, and not a stockbroker, money manager, or anyone with a vested interest in selling you something.

My advice to Lisa was based on the appalling stories I heard from women I interviewed. Wendy, for example, was a single mother who was working hard to support her son. On the urgings of a friend, she invested some of her savings with a stockbroker, a decision she later regretted. "The broker didn't take a long-term look at what my needs and goals were. He never talked to me about allocation of funds," she complained. "He put me way too heavily in limited partnerships. When these investments went down the tube, I realized I wanted a whole plan. I didn't want to get it piecemeal. How come brokers never asked me about the big picture?"

Why indeed? The answer is simple. As financial columnist Herb Greenberg warned, "Do not confuse brokers with planners. Planners create total financial plans; brokers are interested in only one thing—selling securities."

This is where it gets confusing. There are so many people who call themselves financial planners—accountants, bankers, lawyers, insurance agents, real estate or security brokers—but many are simply salespeople looking to make a quick (and big) buck. A person with the initials CFP (Certified Financial Planner) after his or her name has taken courses, passed tests, and met requirements to perform financial planning services. But even those credentials don't guarantee quality. The most important thing to know about financial planners, besides their experience, is how they are paid.

- *Fee only* planners charge on the basis of service and time and have nothing to sell.
- *Commission-only* planners offer their services for free but sell

commission-producing products, such as mutual funds, limited partnerships, insurance products, and stocks and bonds.

- *Fee-plus-commission* planners charge an up-front fee for consultation and their written plan, then charge commissions on the financial products they sell.

My preference, as was the case with most women I interviewed, is a fee-based planner—someone to design an overall plan, which we can either implement ourselves or entrust to the appropriate professional. That's the only way to avoid a conflict of interest. Wendy, for example, finally figured out that her broker was steering her to investments for which he received the biggest commissions. Eventually she switched to a fee-based financial planner. She paid the planner for his time, and then, based on the investment advice he gave her, she bought stocks through a discount brokerage firm.

"How do you find a financial planner?" Lisa asked.

"The same way you've found baby-sitters, hairdressers, or the best schools for your kids," I responded. "By asking people you know." Everyone—from a next-door neighbor to a favorite aunt to the family doctor—is a potential source of referrals. "But be creative," I urged her.

One woman I interviewed didn't know a soul to ask but read about a financial advisor in a magazine. Even though he was out of state, she called and told him she needed help, and he referred her to several financial planners in her area. "I didn't even know there were financial planners," she said chuckling. Yet by the time she finished, she had met with thirteen of them.

Marion is another example. "I asked everyone I knew, including my manicurist. She talks to about two hundred women a week. She would ask her clients for me, Who do you use?"

From the names she collected, Marion narrowed her list to ten people, based on a set of criteria. "My goal was to have someone help me find some mutual funds, really diversify, and keep the money in the funds over a long period of time. I didn't want to go far. The person had to be in the radius of my work and home," she said. "I wanted someone who was fee-based—I didn't want to pay a commission. I would buy the funds directly from the fund companies."

From these ten names, she picked one. "I found a financial planner who charges a flat fee. He helped me pick out funds. He helps me with the paperwork. He helps me think strategy. About every quarter, we sit down and look at how I'm doing. At the end of the year, we might move some things around."

Marion made an interesting observation. The process of searching for financial help is in itself an education. "It was a fascinating four-month process," Marion told me. "As I learned more and more about money, I realized I didn't need to be stupid about this anymore. In fact, I knew a lot more than some of my friends."

When I spoke to Lisa on the phone some time later, I asked how things were going. "Great," she said, clearly thrilled that she had found a "terrific" advisor. "He asks me a lot of questions and gets me going in the right direction," she explained. "He's helped me see all the little steps that I needed to take in order to be fiscally responsible to myself, like paying off my credit card debt and setting up an IRA. He showed me how to do a net worth statement and a cash flow statement, so I could figure out where I was. I've started writing down everything I spend, which forces me to be more aware. He had me look at my insurance, my estate plan, things I never would have thought of before."

The next time she sees him, she told me, they will discuss how much to allocate for retirement, an emergency reserve, and a personal portfolio. "I really see that the structure needs to be in place before I start throwing money in," she said. "You need to have a plan."

How does she feel? "I feel like it's something I can do. My confidence has increased. I am so relieved that I don't have to work longer hours to be able to afford what I want."

Even the most financially adept knew there were times when they needed similar assistance or to modify and update their plans on a regular basis.

I'll never forget a recent phone conversation with Margaret, in which she mentioned casually that she had just made an appointment to see a financial planner. I was surprised. She was, after all, a comptroller, managing the bank's portfolio as well as her family's investments. Why would she need a financial planner?

"I'm worried we aren't doing enough for retirement," she told me. "I want a structure, a plan. My husband thinks we can do it ourselves. Which is true. We can read up on all this stuff, but it takes so much time and effort."

Naomi, who has been an active investor for years, told me how a financial planner helps her and her husband stay on the right financial track. "We do plans every few years. Issues change. We need to reevaluate," she said, explaining the process. "We set out the parameters—we have three kids who need to go to college; this is when we want to retire; this is what we think our business will be worth. We come up with a plan—how much insurance we need, how much savings, a variety of things we need to do. Then we go out and implement it. This plan gives us comfort—we know what we have to do. One of the problems with not having a plan is you think, Oh, my God, am I doing everything I can to take care of my family? It's just another place for discomfort, to feel you're not in control. At least now, if we're not following the plan, we know what we're giving up. It's a conscious choice."

Implementing the Plan

Generally speaking, *fee-only* financial planners rarely do the day-to-day managing of an account. (It's the *commissioned* planner who usually will be the one to actually make the investments.) If we want someone else to actively oversee our investments, then we may want a money manager. After a while, Wendy told me, she switched from a discount broker to a money manager, who managed her portfolio (i.e., he had full authority to make trades in her name) for a quarterly fee based on a percentage of assets managed.

"I like that someone is watching the market and evaluating it more closely than my financial planner did before," Wendy told me. "When I first started with Tom, I just wanted to put the money someplace and leave it there. Now, with Joslyn, it is a little bit more sophisticated. She moves in and out of stocks at different times. I like that Joslyn looks at the stuff with me quarterly. I like that she keeps on top of the holdings. We set up a plan at the beginning of the year, and it's taken six months to implement it."

People who manage money generally have the initials RIA after their name, meaning they are a registered investment advisor. What does it take to become an RIA? Not much. "As long as you haven't committed a crime, the only requirement is that you can fog a mirror," an investment adviser told *Business Week* magazine. Except for a small onetime filing fee, no formal training, experience, exams, or license is required. The lack of regulation in an industry that's growing rapidly means that the onus is on us. We have to stay vigilant, keeping constant tabs on the manager's activity, making sure the account is in our name, that only we have the power to withdraw money.

Professional money managers can be quite pricey. They normally require a minimum initial investment, anywhere from $100,000 to $1 million. If we can't afford to meet their minimum, we can still have a professional overseeing our portfolio. That's the beauty of a good mutual fund. In fact, mutual funds are popular among all income levels. With a mutual fund, we get a diversified basket of stocks managed by a pro. Some funds charge a load (sales fee), others don't. All funds have management fees, but some are heftier than others. My bent is definitely toward no-loads. With good no-load funds, we can have an outstanding money manager for a fraction of the cost.

Depending on the amount we have to invest, we could do a combination of things: put some money with a portfolio manager and some in mutual funds, and invest the rest on our own, perhaps guided by a stockbroker.

"If you hire someone, you can still set aside some money that is not of major consequence and play with it, have fun with it," says financial consultant Joyce Linker. "Almost all of my clients have some money that they invest on their own."

Most women I interviewed consulted a variety of professionals, each of them with a different expertise. "I like having several people to bat around ideas with," said one woman about her tax accountant and stockbroker. Some women actually gathered their advisors together on a regular basis. Lauren was one of them. She was working long hours, traveling weeks on end, and had little time to devote to finances. Her solution: manage her finances the way she managed her company—by assembling a team and delegating.

"I said to my attorney—whom I have total faith in—if I were to put together a team of advisors, what areas do you think I need help in?" Based on that advice, she called her accountant, pension planner, attorney, and financial advisor together for a meeting.

"The first time I put them all together it was awkward. You know how you go to a school dance and you don't know if you should actually dance or not. That's what it was like. But now we all work together as a team. I tell them: 'Nate, if you have a question, call Diane.' I now have them actually calling each other.

"For example, I just got into a real estate deal. When I got a letter from the bank regarding this deal, I faxed it to my advisor, accountant, and attorney, with a note: You three discuss it, and one of you get back to me by such and such date. And they'll do it. It's great. They're terrific."

Another woman is less structured in her approach. "Once a year, I go to my estate lawyer. I come in with a sheet of paper, a summary of what I have, and I ask him, 'Is there anything else I should be doing? If anything should happen to me, are my kids protected?' I take the same piece of paper, go to my accountant, and say to him, 'This is what I have and this is where it is. Is there anything taxwise I should be doing differently?' Then our lawyer and accountant talk to each other if they need to."

Another woman told me, "I actually play my brother, who is a stockbroker, and my financial planner against each other. I have each of them recommend five or six different funds in each category, like five real estate partnerships and five different bond funds. Then I go to the other one and ask what he thinks of the list. I do the same with my father. Sometimes I call the accountant and ask him questions and my lawyer and ask him questions. I feel good about the advice I've gotten."

Should I See a Financial Planner?

● ● ● ● ● ● ● ● ● ● ● ● ● ●

Are you wondering if you should consult a financial planner? Read this list and check any statements that describe your situation. If any of these apply to you, you're a good candidate for financial planning and professional advice.

- ☐ 1. I am in debt and can't seem to get out.
- ☐ 2. I am too busy. I have no time to manage money.
- ☐ 3. I have gotten involved with some bad investments, and I'm concerned.
- ☐ 4. I keep trying to learn about money, but I can't seem to get anywhere.
- ☐ 5. I want to take charge of my money, but I have no confidence in myself.
- ☐ 6. My spouse/partner and I constantly argue about what to do with our money, so we end up doing nothing.
- ☐ 7. I don't have a cent in savings and can barely make ends meet.
- ☐ 8. I don't have a retirement plan.
- ☐ 9. I have a 401(k) plan, but I don't understand what's in it or if it is invested well. Or: Only my husband has a retirement plan, but neither of us understands what's in it or if it's invested well.
- ☐ 10. I don't have insurance. Or: I don't know if I have enough.
- ☐ 11. I don't have an estate plan or a will. Or: I'm not sure if I've adequately prepared for my heirs.
- ☐ 12. I have a specific goal in mind (a new car, a second house). How can I achieve it?
- ☐ 13. I want to make a change in my life (start a family, switch careers). Can I afford it?
- ☐ 14. I see a change in lifestyle looming (a divorce, a marriage, a cross-country move). How do I prepare for it?
- ☐ 15. Someone else, my husband or a money manager, takes care of my money. I am in the dark. I'm not even sure what are the right questions to ask.
- ☐ 16. I have or expect to come into money (an inheritance, a bonus, a pay raise).
- ☐ 17. I have all my money in a savings account.

● ● ● ● ● ● ● ● ● ● ● ● ● ●

Lessons from Those Who Have Been There

Not all professionals are knowledgeable, trustworthy, or qualified. "I've gotten into a lot of trouble listening to other people," sobbed a woman who lost virtually everything by following the advice of a highly touted professional. "That's the scariest part. How do you find help you can trust?"

It wasn't uncommon, among the women I interviewed, to find advisors who inadvertently misled or purposefully deceived them. In truth, financial professionals can be wonderful tutors. They can also be unconscionable scoundrels. They can be godsends or charlatans, saviors or swindlers. In these women's stories are a number of lessons we can learn and precautions we can take to make sure we find the right people.

"Fifteen years ago," one woman told me, "I got a phone call from a guy who had been a teacher and became a broker, and I just felt sorry for him. My husband and I each gave him about $1,000. I pulled out after he lost the first $100. My husband lost almost the whole $1,000 before he pulled out. I realized you can feel sorry for someone over the phone, but you don't give him your money." *Lesson #1: Never, ever give money blindly to anyone, even a friend, and especially not to a stranger on the phone.*

"Anyone can put up a shingle as a financial professional," Joyce Linker told me. "It's a needed service. But it's hard to find someone good. You have to be a very good detective."

Lesson #2: Before you decide on an advisor, interview at least three professionals and check out their qualifications. When I asked Marion how she narrowed down her list of ten names, she responded, "I made a list of questions and I systematically interviewed each person, asking each those same questions. I come from a family where my mother told me it never hurts to ask; all people can say is *no*. I also came in with a list of all my assets and all my husband's assets, and I put it right there on the table. And I'd say, How can you help me? Then I used my gut-level reaction as to whether I trusted them or not."

What kind of questions should we ask? "Ask whatever questions you want," urges Joyce Linker. "It's your money and your decision. You have a right to ask anything. They expect it. If you want to know why they sit funny in their chair, you can ask."

Another financial advisor, Ann Lieberman, told me, "Some people come in without a question in mind. I think it's a good idea to go in with specific questions. How do you compare if you don't have criteria, if you don't use the same list of questions with each person? I had two clients this week who walked in with the list of questions from *Personal Finance for Dummies*. One of them asked me each question, one by one; the other handed me the list and said, 'Answer them.' "

My friend Lisa interviewed three financial planners before she made her choice.

"How did it go?" I asked her later.

"I was sort of dazed," she said, describing her first interview. "I couldn't believe I was doing it. I was embarrassed because I felt so dumb. Also I was skeptical. Could I trust him? I was more in a sensing mode. How did I feel with him?"

By the time she interviewed the third planner, she said, "I had a better sense of what I needed to know. I was more specific in my questions. And he was clearer in his explanations."

Lesson #3: Despite good intentions, not everyone has our best interests in mind. For example, Wendy told me her boyfriend's advice: "He'd say, 'Good God, you have enough money that you could probably spend as much as you wanted for the rest of your life and still have money left. Why do you worry about this?' But if I had kept spending at the level he wanted, I wouldn't have had any left."

I'll never forget the hysterical phone call I got from Gayle, the successful writer with no retirement plan, who had just completed a class taught by a financial planner. She was so impressed with the teacher's knowledge, she gave him her entire savings to put in an IRA. Two months later, she was short $3,000. The market, meanwhile, had soared 9 percent. "What's going on?" she wondered in absolute panic. It turned out that in a rush to ease the anxiety over her retirement, she had thrown caution to the wind. "I trusted a charming stranger without checking references or fully understanding his proposed plan," she confessed. This "charming stranger" not only put her money in funds that charged outrageously high loads, but he charged her a management fee on top of that. All those fees took a $3,000 bite out of her principal. To make matters worse, the investments were horribly diversified for an IRA, too heavily weighted in bonds and cash.

"How did I do such a stupid thing?" she wailed. "I assumed that anyone who taught a financial class at the Women's Center would be good and honorable. And I assumed that engaging a financial planner meant you were hiring someone who would look out for your best interests."

In this business, assumptions are dangerous.

Lesson #4: Knowledge is our best safeguard against deception, misguidance, or stupid mistakes. No matter how well-meaning our family, or how smart our friends, or how highly regarded is an expert, we must be informed enough to evaluate what they tell us. Whether we follow our spouse's suggestions or a newsletter's recommendations, or we employ professionals, we must become educated enough to assess their advice and monitor their performance.

"I didn't have enough knowledge," Gayle admitted, as we tried to analyze what went wrong with the financial planner she used. "I think I assumed unconsciously that anything I didn't understand didn't apply to me. Now that I look at his brochure more carefully, if I had understood what 'How we get paid' meant, I might have anticipated this happening."

Lesson #5: When someone claims to have a "sure thing" or pressures us to act quickly before it's too late, go somewhere else. In the investment world, there is no such thing as a "sure thing." "If stockbrokers know so much," a friend once said, "how come they aren't all millionaires?" Besides, if we miss one good investment, there is always another.

Lesson #6: Meet with advisors on a regular basis, ask a lot of questions, and make sure we understand the answers. Once we hire a professional, we must stay alert. "You can't just say, 'Here it is and good-bye,'" one woman insisted. "You really have to take an interest." It was a painful lesson for Gayle. "I assumed that a financial planner would *make sure* that you *understood* what he was doing and what it would cost you before taking action," she lamented. Smart women know the burden of understanding is on them.

"I must drive him nuts with all my questions," Marion told me of her financial advisor. "If I don't understand something, I always say, 'Slow down. I don't get it. Tell it to me again.'"

"You have to be a good client," explained Joyce Linker. "I get really surprised when I ask people if they are paying a fee based on their assets and they don't know. Or I ask is this a discretionary account? If they don't know, they are not good clients. They aren't informed. That's part of understanding. If you can't remember things, you write it down. If someone asked me what the fee was for each of my managers, I don't know. But I know where it's written down."

Lesson #7: Keep close tabs on what the advisor's doing. Several years ago, I found a stockbroker I liked a lot. I gave him discretionary control over my account. He called me regularly with glowing reports, and almost daily I received transaction slips for trades he was making. At first I read everything he sent me. But after a while I got lazy.

One day, watching me drop another transaction slip atop the growing pile on my desk, Cal, my husband-to-be, asked, "What are all those?" I handed him the stack, and he leafed through it, then looked at me in amazement. "Do you realize this guy is churning your account?" he exclaimed. "He's making excessive trades, investing in highly speculative options, racking up outrageous commissions—he's even buying on margin!"

I was shocked. It turned out a man I thought had the Midas touch was no better than a riverboat gambler. This is not uncommon in the brokerage industry. According to Dr. Marvin Steinburg, a psychiatrist who heads the Connecticut Council on Compulsive Gambling, too many brokers are actually "unrecognized problem gamblers." It may be common, but I felt like an idiot. It would be the last time I'd ever relinquish responsibility—but it took a sledgehammer to wake me up.

Which brings us to another critical point. *Lesson #8: When dissatisfied, change advisors.* Obviously, if our advisor's performance is not up to par, we want to find out what's going on, and if his or her explanations don't satisfy us, then we should switch. But an equally good reason for change is if we feel intimidated or poorly treated. Women are particularly vulnerable. "The brokerage business is a macho business," a former broker told the *Wall Street Journal*. Studies show that banks and brokerage firms are notorious for giving women less information, time, and respect than men. If we happen to run into someone who treats us as though we're stupid, we should, without a doubt, find someone else.

Gayle not only fired the "charming stranger" who was her financial advisor; she consulted her accountant, plus two other financial advisors, and, with their help, was able to get her total investment returned, recouping all losses. She's also developed a smarter strategy. She's interviewing a number of financial consultants, finding "financial buddies" whom she checks in with before making any decisions, and has started a financial self-help support group at the same Women's Center where she took the class. This time, she vows, "I'm not going to be in such a hurry. I'm going to move carefully, not emotionally."

The Most Important Lesson of All

Not long ago, I was having lunch with my friend Lisa, and we got around to discussing her financial advisor. "I have to tell you something, Barbara," she confessed awkwardly, then hesitated, obviously embarrassed. "When I first walked into his office, I immediately saw him as a father. I wanted to say to him, 'Just take it, do it all for me.'" Fortunately, she recognized the fantasy and snapped out of it immediately. "I felt like a sleeping princess awakening," she said, laughing.

Her metaphor couldn't have been more appropriate. *Lesson #9: Financial professionals make lousy Prince Charmings.* We can't afford to sleepwalk into anyone's office. Unless we're wide awake, we could fall into a familiar and dangerous trap. I call it the Surrogate Syndrome. This is exactly what happened when I gave Bob Lovett, the money manager I found, my money to invest. I felt so grown up making my first independent financial decision. But it was a sham, a ruse, a pretense. I was just switching Prince Charmings. I fired a spouse and hired an advisor. I was masquerading as an independent woman, but in truth, I was still operating in a state of childlike dependency. Bob became my surrogate prince. I not only gave him my money; I handed him my power as well.

Whether someone else has discretionary control over our money or we're simply following advice, eschewing responsibility is *always, always, always* an act of self-sabotage. Trusting someone else to "do it all for me," as my friend almost did, leaves us vulnerable and unprotected should something happen to that someone else or to our portfolio.

Luckily, Bob was honest and quite successful. But not all experts are so ethical. "My stockbroker kept telling me how great we were doing," one woman recalled. "After a year and a half, I sat down and tried to figure it out. I was stunned when I saw that my initial investment of $116,900 was now worth just over $60,000. And I had paid him $5,600 in commissions for screwing up."

This woman is not alone. There are countless stories of supposedly reputable experts ripping off unwitting individuals. Charles Givens is a financial guru whose books are still big sellers. Yet he was found guilty by a jury for giving advice that left one follower nearly destitute. Then there were the two hotshot financial advisors who hosted syndicated radio shows—one out of Los Angeles, the other from New York—both of whom were indicted on multiple counts of fraud for bilking investors out of over $30 million. Even first-rate brokerage firms have paid out more than $10 million in the past three years for mishandling clients' accounts.

Marion, seeing how uninformed her friends were, finally realized that no one cared about saving her money and increasing her net worth more than she did.

"A lot of my friends just let other people control their money," she told me. "I would ask them simple questions like who do you use and what do you pay them? And they didn't know. One person told me she was really happy with her money manager. I asked her the guy's fee. She said three percent [of her assets]. I said, Isn't that an awful lot? She said no. I asked how much return on her investment she got, and she said about ten percent. I said, Well, subtract three percent, and you're making seven percent. Then subtract taxes. You're just a couple of points away from inflation. Are you happy about that? She said, Gee, I hadn't thought about it that way.

"I also heard horror stories," Marion continued. "I spoke to a couple who gave their money to this professor who taught courses on money. He was in every college brochure, he was very visible. But he ran off with everybody's money, including theirs. Other friends told me about giving $800,000 to some big fancy investment firm in New York, and by the end of the year they had $400,000. They were retired. The firm put their retirement money in junk bonds."

The Journey Continues

All that we've learned thus far will help protect us from deception and needless loss. Indeed, we have come a long way in this heroic journey to financial responsibility. And it should be comforting to know that we don't need to travel this path alone. There are people waiting to help us all along the way. By the time we've reached this sixth realization, many of us recognize how savvy we've become. Still, we're not yet at journey's end. There is much more in store for us. As we're about to discover, these six realizations are leading us to an expanded, and perhaps unexpected, panorama. In the final part, The Power, we'll see that the path we're on goes far beyond financial success.

••• **CHAPTER EIGHT RECAPPED** •••

Realization Even though money is considered a private matter, nothing could be more damaging to our financial health than this "no talk" rule. Getting smart with money does not occur in a vacuum. We must reach out, talk to family and friends, consult with experts, get support, learn from others, and seek the services of financial professionals.

To Do
1. Do the checklist on p. 160.
2. Find a financial planner. Start by talking to people and gathering names. Interview at least three advisors. Ask them for references. Be sure and call those references before making any decisions.

In Search of an Advisor/Questions to Ask

The following questions are compiled from two sources: Marion's list of questions she used during her research; and a booklet I coauthored, "Choosing and Managing Financial Professionals," published by Resourceful Women.

Questions to ask friends, family, people you can talk to about managing money:

(1) What do you invest in?

(2) How did you learn about money and investing?

(3) Does anyone help you invest? Are you satisfied with him/her? Does that person educate you? How does he or she charge?

(4) What is your level of risk?

(5) Whom would you recommend I talk to?

(6) What are some mistakes you've made?

(7) What advice would you give me?

Before you meet with a financial consultant, ask yourself these questions:

(1) What is my net worth?

(2) How much money do I have to invest?

(3) What are my financial goals? Are they the same as my partner's?

(4) How do my goals rank on a scale of 1 through 10? Does my partner have similar priorities?

(5) What kinds of risks am I willing to take?

(6) What do I want from a financial advisor?

(7) What should an advisor know about me?

Questions to ask a financial professional (their answers will vary, depending on whether the advisor is a money manager actually managing your money, a stockbroker helping you invest, or a financial planner devising a strategy):

(1) Will you tell me about your education, experience, investment philosophy, and past performance?

(2) Do you specialize in certain investments?

(3) Can I talk to some of your clients, particularly those with financial circumstances similar to mine?

(4) What services can I expect from you? (Will you design a plan for me? Will you help me implement it?)

(5) Do you, or does someone on your staff, communicate with clients? How often?

(6) How are you compensated for your services? (If by fees, what do your fees include? If by commission, how much will that cost me?)

(7) Are you registered with the Securities and Exchange Commission? May I see a copy of SEC Form ADV Part II, which lists any disciplinary actions regulators have taken against you?

(8) Is there anything else I should know about you?

3. Make an appointment with a financial advisor to prepare a financial plan or update the one you have. This is not just for investing but to look

at your insurance coverage, financial goals, debt repayment, estate and retirement plans.

4. Implement your plan. You have a number of choices regarding investments.

- A stockbroker. Either a full-service broker, who will give you advice in exchange for a higher commission, or a discount broker, where you're on your own.
- A money manager. He or she makes the investment decisions and executes the trades.
- Mutual fund companies. You buy direct from the fund distributor.
- Dividend reinvestment plans. You can buy stock directly from certain companies. Call the company's investor relations department. A very good resource: *No-Load Stocks: How to Buy Your First Share and Every Share Directly from the Company with No Broker's Fee*, by Charles B. Carlson.

5. Read "Choosing and Managing Financial Professionals: A Guide for Women Investors," by Deanne Stone and Barbara Stanny. You can order it from Resourceful Women, Presidio Building 1016, P.O. Box 29423, San Francisco, CA 94129-0423. It's a very readable, comprehensive, and uncomplicated booklet, if I say so myself!

• •

Part Three

THE POWER

When a woman uses her money to express her values and beliefs, when she makes financial decisions based on *who she is,* not on what she *should* do, and when she acts firmly and confidently on those decisions, then she becomes a very powerful woman. It is here that she comes to the seventh and final realization: **I can make a difference.** As more and more powerful, fully realized women reach this point, all of humanity stands to benefit. "When it comes to saving the world or part of it," write Patricia Aburdene and John Naisbett in *Megatrends for Women,* "women are the catalyst through whom the critical mass for social change will be achieved."

Chapter Nine

• •

The Financially Savvy Woman

*What the caterpillar calls the end of the world,
the master calls a butterfly.*
—ANONYMOUS

Now What?

We have, in the preceding pages, traveled a path to financial responsibility. While the journey has been mapped out, realization by realization, we know the map is not the territory.

For many, accepting the teachings of each realization and following the suggestions at the end of each chapter have been sufficient enough to get you going. You have a sense of how to start and what to do next. The process is well under way, or at the very least it seems feasible. Financial fluency appears attainable. To gauge how far you've come, refer back to the questionnaire that you filled in earlier (page xxi), and take it again. You'll very likely see you've made progress . . . perhaps more than you realize.

But some of you may still be wondering: How does all this work in real life? How do I put these realizations into action? Where do I begin? You may still be confused, unsure what to do, and your new score on the questionnaire reflects your need for further assistance. The easy answer would be to say: Just follow the realizations in their order of presentation. But in truth, integrating the *inner work* of individuation, education, and self-awareness with the *outer work* of uncovering "secrets," taking risks, and seeking help doesn't always occur in a rigid sequence. For some of us, the process is not that neat and tidy. Everyone's situation is different. Where we start depends on where we are.

Those of you who feel financially proficient, or at least are heading in that direction, might want to skip to "The Beat Goes On," on page 177.

If, however, you still feel unsure or confused, take a moment to complete the following checklist. Its purpose is to help assess your situation and, from there, determine the most appropriate starting point.

Where Do I Go Now?

• • • • • • • • • • • • • •

Check the box, or boxes, that best describe how you currently feel.

☐ 1. I still find this whole subject terribly confusing.

☐ 2. I am very afraid of making a mistake and losing everything.

☐ 3. I feel stuck and don't know why.

☐ 4. I am eager but uninformed.

☐ 5. I am knowledgeable but have some concerns.

☐ 6. I have invested in the past but lately find myself postponing any financial decisions.

☐ 7. I am struggling with (or distracted by) some painful issues that have nothing to do with money.

☐ 8. Truthfully, I don't want the risk or responsibility of handling money. I want someone else to do it.

☐ 9. No matter what I do, I can't seem to make any progress.

• • • • • • • • • • • • • •

*Uninformed? Confused? Trouble getting going? Start
with Realization #6, I don't have to do this alone.*

If you checked boxes 1, 2, or 3, find an advisor, preferably a financial
planner. Remember, *You don't have to do this alone!* Read Chapter
Eight again, start collecting names, then make an appointment to interview at least three professionals. The truth of the matter is that for most
people, Realization #6 is truly the best place to begin.

*No trouble absorbing financial information? Start
with Realization #2, Learning follows a curve.*

Does this mean we should all visit a financial planner first thing? Certainly
not. Every one of us can benefit from expert advice. But if you checked
boxes 4, 5, or 6, you could certainly begin by doing some research on
your own.

Lots of women I interviewed much preferred to educate themselves.
These do-it-yourself types went straight to Realization #2, *Learning follows a curve.* They started by picking up a book, attending a lecture, or
taking a class, and just kept going from there. This is particularly true for
women with a financial background or an avid interest in the subject.

"Investing was easy for me to understand," Margaret told me. "I was an
accounting major and a CPA. That helped a lot."

Marion, on the other hand, who felt "totally stupid" when she began, intended to use a financial planner. But in the process of looking for
one, she educated herself. And the professionals she interviewed were
charging a fortune for what she described as a "glitzy pie chart of an
anonymous John E. Example shot out of a colored printer. These are real
showy and impressive for a novice," she told me. "But I asked, 'What computer program is that?' And they told me. I went over to Computerware
and looked up some programs that would calculate how long it would take
me to retire and would let me plug in my financials to see an asset allocation pie chart. I bought a program for $49. It was very straightforward.
These people I had been talking to wanted to charge me anywhere from
$2,500 to $8,000, depending on their overhead. I even asked one guy,

'Couldn't I do this myself if I got the right software?' He said, 'You could if you want to spend time plugging in the numbers.' "

Procrastinating? Avoiding? Forgetting? Start with Realization #3, All the answers aren't out there.

Of course, even the best intentions often go astray. What if, as motivated as you may feel, you're still having difficulty making decisions or taking action? Most likely, the problems you're experiencing have a psychological source that has nothing to do with money itself.

If you checked box 7, 8, or 9, or if you've tried everything and still feel stuck, then dealing with underlying issues should be your first task. Reread Chapter Five and spend some time doing the inner work. Unless you break through internal barriers, perhaps by way of therapy or a support group, you'll have a difficult time making any significant progress with your finances.

Ready to roll? Incorporating Realization #4, There are no secrets, and Realization #5, Risk is not a synonym for loss.

The reason for resistance may have nothing to do with any emotional baggage. Sometimes it is simple inertia. If you checked box 5 or 6, you're educated, even experienced, but for some reason, defer making decisions. You may just need to do something. Financial inertia usually stems from fear of the unknown, which translates into fear of loss. The best antidote to this kind of inertia is action. I remember Sonya, an astute insurance executive, who received a large bonus when the market was at an all-time high. Convinced stocks were headed for a fall, she stood by while the Dow-Jones index continued to climb.

We talked at length about her paralysis. "Maybe I'm one of those women who are waiting for their prince," she suggested.

"I doubt it," I countered, familiar with her market savvy. She later called to tell me I was right.

"I wasn't waiting for a man," she admitted. "I was sitting in the wings, waiting for the market to correct. Finally I said, 'Get in there, Sonya. You can't time it. Just do it.'"

This is a common problem. A lot of people are waiting for the perfect time to enter the market. Sonya thought she might be jeopardizing her windfall if she invested at the wrong time. It wasn't until she hit upon Realization #4, *There are no secrets,* that she was able to acknowledge, "You can't time it," which freed her to "get in there." From past experience, she understood Realization #5, *Risk is not a synonym for loss,* and she was able to "just do it."

How did she do it? "I started with a small amount," she told me, "and went up the investment pyramid, putting in little bits at each level. When I had some success, it became easier."

The Beat Goes On

Once we've begun, the journey never really ends. Financial responsibility is an ongoing process. Just because we've gained some finesse doesn't mean we can fall asleep at the wheel. *Smart women understand that getting smart is important but staying smart is vital.* I learned two indispensable lessons from women I interviewed.

The first lesson: Keep track of your investments

"My game plan," one woman told me, "is to keep my money where it is. Look at it every few months. Keep getting more savvy about the money game."

Remember Gayle, who lost $3,000 right off the bat when she gave money to an advisor to manage? She saved herself from even further and bigger losses because she carefully read her statements. Immediately, when she saw her balance was shrinking, she did something about it. Smart women keep a watchful eye on their money, regularly tracking their investments. Monitoring money does *not* have to consume us. Some women told me they dedicated a certain number of hours each week, even daily, to this task. The majority, financial professionals included, devoted much less time to their finances, updating their portfolios on a monthly or quarterly basis.

"I don't look at my stuff every day, not even every month," Linda Pei, who runs a mutual fund, told me. "First, who has the time? Second, with the jumps up and down, it'll scare you to death. I pretty much look at it once every six months and then analyze everything at the end of the year."

Phyllis, a stockbroker, told me the same thing. "I get a statement every quarter. I may change things once a year. I don't look at my investments on a daily basis."

Joyce, a financial consultant who invests with a number of money managers, "throws everything they send me into the file," she explains, "and I update it every quarter." How? "I keep a spread sheet," she said. "However, if I were more computer literate, it would be on the computer. I track the performances of my funds and the beginning and ending balances. I have quarter returns, year-to-date returns, ending balance, and any withdrawals and deposits."

The second lesson: This is not an exercise in perfection

Our goal is to become financially responsible, not flawless or irreproachable. The women I interviewed were extremely competent, but not one of them was infallible, nor were their actions always impeccable. We've mentioned this before, but it bears repeating. There is a tendency among women to berate ourselves unmercifully for anything less than perfection. But that's a self-defeating trap. It's the prime way we incapacitate ourselves, undermine our efforts, and forestall any further progress. Even the smartest women can sabotage their success if they're not careful.

Do you have any difficulties with this stuff? I often asked women, for my own reassurance more than anything else. Not one woman responded *no*. More often, they answered like Joyce. "Oh, sure. I do the usual stuff. Procrastinate. Ignore things. I probably should have left one of my managers, but I haven't. I'm like everyone else. I'm afraid I'll get out and this will be his best year."

Joyce was fully aware of her imperfections, the folly of some of her actions, the insecurity she couldn't completely shake, but she remained diligent and responsible to the best of her ability. She didn't let temporary setbacks become long-term slumps.

Whether we're just starting out or well on our way, we can summarize so much of what's been said with the following pieces of advice. I call them the *Seven Pointers for Starting Out and Staying on Track:*

1. You don't have to have it all together. Just start.
2. It's okay not to know, as long as you're willing to learn.
3. If in doubt, reach out. Get support.
4. There are no stupid questions. Just make sure you understand the answers.
5. Stay informed. Update your portfolio regularly.
6. Progress, not perfection, is the goal.
7. Mistakes and losses are always opportunities for learning.

With these pointers in mind, and the six realizations under our belt, we can't help but grow consistently smarter in relationship to money. But that's only part of what we can expect. Where does all this lead? You may be surprised.

Becoming Our Realizations

As our journey progresses, eventually we may notice that something more subtle, though no less significant, is beginning to take place—a process within a process. I once read, though I've forgotten where, that change happens in three stages: *awareness, understanding,* and *action.* Indeed, as we become *aware* of the realizations, start to really *understand* what they mean, and then begin to *act* on them, a profound shift occurs within us.

When we integrate the realizations into our thinking, our belief system changes. And as our beliefs change, we change. Like a sponge immersed in water, we actually *absorb* the primary characteristic of each realization. We not only follow the guidelines inherent in the realizations; we in fact *take on* the essence of the realizations themselves. Put another way, the six realizations we've learned so far, which have given us the steps to getting there, are also the qualities of being there.

These six qualities make up what I believe are the principal traits that typify a financially responsible woman. They were certainly evident in every woman I interviewed. These six fundamental characteristics, when combined, constitute what I regard as the *essential spirit of the smart woman*. A financially smart woman is:

- **Self-reliant**—She is capable of making autonomous decisions.
- **Financially informed**—She is educated and well versed in the subject.
- **Personally aware**—She is continually examining her internal barriers and resources.
- **Self-assured**—She is not intimidated by the mystique around money.
- **A risk taker**—She is willing take a certain amount of risk to reap the financial rewards.
- **Interdependent**—She is quick to seek help, support, and guidance.

The Seventh Characteristic

There's more. The confluence of these six characteristics creates a powerful alchemy: *Awareness* coupled with *understanding* produces knowledge. *Understanding* followed by *action* leads to wisdom. A smart woman turns into a wise woman. What's the difference? A smart woman has learned to take charge of her money. A wise woman has learned to take charge of her life. She has the wisdom to make discerning choices.

This was an unexpected lesson I learned from the women I interviewed. The knowledge to invest wisely is merely the first part of taking financial responsibility. The other part, equally important, is the wisdom to use money in a meaningful way. This gives us the seventh characteristic of a financially responsible woman: **Powerful**.

• • •

Early on, I declared that this book is about far more than money. It is about power, personal power. Taking financial responsibility is more than learning the lingo or making a few bucks. Taking financial responsibility is a transformational experience that empowers us personally as well as enhances us financially. As we noted in Chapter Two, money, despite the clichés, is not power. Power, by definition, is the ability to act, to get things done. The word comes from the Old French *poeir*, which means "to be able." *Money, by itself, is not able to do anything.*

As management consultant Bonnie Lampton so aptly put it during our interview, "If I put $1,000 on this desk and turn off the light, nothing will happen. Money has *no* ability to produce action."

But *we* do. This is an important distinction. We become powerful not by the amount of money we have but by the choices we make and the actions we take. Being able to buy fancy cars or designer dresses is not in itself a measure of power. But when money becomes a tool for self-expression and a source of self-fulfillment, then a woman is truly empowered. A wise woman who makes fulfilling choices becomes an unquestionably powerful woman.

Indeed, I considered the women I interviewed quite powerful women. They spoke with confidence and self-assurance about who they were and what they wanted. That's not to say that their lives were without problems. But they knew they had choices. Furthermore, they knew that they, and no one else, were in charge of and responsible for those choices, and as best they could, they were making choices that reflected their personal values. Certainly, they had their moments—many moments, in fact—when their confidence waned, their self-assurance cracked, and they were filled with self-doubt, if not sheer terror. Yet in spite of their trepidation and regardless of their net worth, they were actively seeking self-determination, financial proficiency, and personal well-being.

Was it the money that empowered them? I think not. It was the process we've described, a combination of the inner work and the outer work, a journey that takes us far beyond a well-financed retirement. The process becomes a transformative experience in which we replace old scripts and antiquated beliefs with our deepest and truest values, dreams, and visions. This is the heroine's journey that takes us from dependency to autonomy, from frustration to fulfillment, a journey that, in the end, puts us in touch with our passion, our potential, and our power. "The hero's journey is the search to find within ourselves the resources to meet our own destiny," Joseph Campbell once explained.

The women I interviewed ran the gamut of personality types and economic backgrounds. But the process they went through, as described in this book, gave them each something money alone could not provide. They had gained control: not control over others, but control over their own lives.

"Money has helped me improve my life," one woman told me. "I've moved, bought a new home, started a new career. But money is a resource. It was up to me to find the courage to do that. Money is only a resource. It can be one of the things that make life easier, but ultimately you've got to chart the course yourself, and make the decisions that make you happy."

Asking the Crucial Question

At what point does a smart woman become a wise woman, and a wise woman a powerful woman? When she knows what she wants and acts on it. How do we make this passage—from awareness and understanding to wisdom and power? By asking ourselves the crucial question "What do I want?" and then taking the answer to heart, using our money as a means to achieve it.

What do I want? This one question can become a potent force for personal change, a bulwark against confusion and helplessness. *What do I want?* It is an ongoing question, to be sure, and the answers will certainly change over a lifetime. But this question provides us with the raw material for carving out meaningful goals and making appropriate decisions, and it becomes the very core of a good financial plan as well as the foundation for a life well lived.

A Question Never Asked

For many women, however, this is not an easy question to answer. Aside from little, if any, experience handling money, we've rarely, if ever, stopped and asked ourselves: "What do I want?" let alone: "How can my money enable me to have what I want?" Historically, we've let something (cultural taboos) or someone (our parents or a spouse) control our lives by determining our decisions. But this has been deadly. Under this system, we lose ourselves. We gradually don't know what we think or what we want anymore. We become scared, angry, resentful. Making simple decisions can become complicated and confusing.

"There is a real phenomenon we've seen among women's psyches," Chris Hayes, of the National Center for Women and Retirement Research, told me. "Women are so used to being caregivers, taking care of others. They don't look at 'What do I need? What do I want?' Women are socialized not to ask these questions."

"If no one has ever asked you what you wanted before, this is not easy," agreed family therapist Judy Barber. "I see my role as a continuing reminder: What do you want?" Which is what we must start doing for ourselves, reminding ourselves continually: What do I want? What are my goals?

According to Kate Levinson, a psychologist who wrote her dissertation on women and money, this is one of the major hurdles women face when taking charge of their finances. "I encourage women I see to take themselves seriously, to use money to make their life meaningful," she told me. "I believe so much of their struggle with money boils down to this issue. The tragic cases are women who feel they have to live their parents' life or deny themselves. They can't use money to have a good life."

When we deny ourselves, we are giving away our power. We become helpless victims. A powerless woman is neither charting her own course nor making decisions that lead her to happiness. And there are a lot of women in this predicament. In a 1994 Harris poll, 61 percent of the women surveyed said they felt powerless. It doesn't make a whit of difference how much money these women have. Powerlessness occurs for one simple reason—we let something or someone else make decisions for us.

If our choices are based on a course someone else charted, if we are doing what others think we *should* do, we are giving our power away.

Why do so many women give their power away? "They're afraid to rock the boat," explained Linda Moore, author of *Release from Powerlessness*. But like a deal with the devil, we pay a high price for this questionable peace. "The basic way we give power away is through dishonesty, not being true to ourselves, not saying what we need," she said. If we can give our power away, however, we can take it back again. And we begin taking our power back the moment we ask ourselves "What do I want?" and then act on that awareness.

Identifying the Goal

I'll never forget one woman, a successful but hard-driven entrepreneur, telling me how she woke up one morning in great emotional pain. "Where is the real me in all of this?" she asked herself fervently. "What about the quality of my life?"

She realized that her success was giving her no pleasure. In time, she saw where that came from. "Enjoyment used to be a no-no in my family," she said. "I can still hear my mother saying, 'Do you really need that?' I would go through my life asking myself that question. Of course, the answer was *no*."

Her goal, she told me, was to use money to live life on her terms, not her parents'. "The journey for me was not to feel guilty about spending money, to enjoy my money."

Other women resurrected long-held dreams in the process of asking the question "What do I want?" One woman told me, "I had taught school, gone back to grad school, worked in banking and retail, but I still wasn't happy. I stopped blaming myself and realized all I ever wanted was to have my own business."

"What happened?" I asked her. "I began to take money more seriously," she replied. "I paid off all my debts, saved up a year's salary, and started my own company. Once I got very intentional about what I wanted, things happened faster. It was really amazing. I even wrote a book."

The answer to "What do I want?" provides us with not only a purposeful goal but also a sense of our priorities, which makes decisions so much easier. One woman told a story that summed up how personal priorities can help us make relevant choices. "Steve and I have a goal," said the forty-six-year-old professional. "We want to be financially independent by the time we're fifty-five. So we know how much we have to save every year. Last year Steve suggested we go on a cruise to celebrate our wedding anniversary. I said I'd love to but it's not more important to me than meeting our savings goal. So we sat down and laid it all out, and it wasn't a problem. I said, 'Let's go.' We really enjoyed ourselves, because we didn't have some vague worry that we were doing something we couldn't afford."

Virtually every woman told me something similar. "I think that the secret to managing money is understanding that you work toward certain goals," Naomi explained. "You have to make a certain set of choices based on those goals. Once I realized this, I was able to settle down and recognize when I'm not doing what I need to do. I understand I have certain choices about money and what that means in terms of trade-offs."

Having a goal and setting priorities is equally important for making investment decisions. So many women, confused by all the choices they had, or by everyone offering conflicting advice, sat down and drew up a kind of shopping list of what they felt was important. Then, when they felt bogged down, overwhelmed by all the options, or questioned a selection, they would refer back to their list of criteria. Again, this exercise begins with that all-important question: "What do I want?"

A woman named Michal explained what she did. "After I had done some research, read some stuff, taken a class or two, I sat down with a book and figured my net worth. I said to myself, Okay, I am going to invest some of this money, so what do I want?" She began jotting down her list. "I want to preserve my capital. I don't want to take big risks, but I'll take moderate ones. I'd like to grow my money ten percent a year. I want diversification. I want socially useful investments. And I don't want to spend any more than five hours a week on getting this whole thing up and running and five hours a month thereafter." Indeed, over the past twenty years, Michal told me, she's averaged 15 to 20 percent a year, putting no more than a few hours a month into managing her funds.

An Unexpected Discovery

It's been a stunning discovery for me to see what happens when women become empowered by the process of taking responsibility. It's not just that they become savvy, or self-reliant, or impressively knowledgeable, or financially wealthy. It isn't just that they're able to make fulfilling choices, create a secure future, or attain meaningful goals. What is most striking is what women do once they've completed the journey, once they've become active in managing their money.

In so many of these women's stories, I heard echoes of what the attorney and feminist activist Anita Hill once told an audience. "We've found our voices," she said, her own voice booming. "Now let's speak on our own terms." It was a stirring challenge to those of us who came to hear her. It's a compelling call for women everywhere. When a woman discovers her own voice and begins speaking on her own terms, something unexpectedly profound occurs.

Not only has she become individually powerful, but she becomes a potent influence in the world around her. In her capacity to make choices, she gains the power to effect change. It is at this point that she finds herself at the seventh realization. When enough women collectively embrace the seventh and final realization, they will have the resources to—quite literally—change the world.

••• CHAPTER NINE RECAPPED •••

In the beginning of this book, we spoke of seven realizations. Thus far we have covered only six. These six realizations are, in fact, all we need to become financially savvy. The steps to getting there are also the qualities of being there. However, once we start taking control of our money, our next challenge is to take control of our life. We do this by making meaningful, personally fulfilling choices. To this end we must continually ask ourselves the crucial question: What do I want? As we find the answers, and act upon them, smart women become wise women. And, in our wisdom, we become powerful. With this, we've laid the groundwork for the seventh, and final, realization.

To Do

1. Ask yourself: *What do I want?* every day for two weeks. Pose the question before you make any decisions, financial or otherwise. Ask it at random about life in general. Be mindful of your responses. Keep a journal of your reactions. Do your answers change with time? Are they consistent? Does anything surprise you? Then observe your behavior and ask yourself: Am I using money in ways that reflect *my* needs, desires, and values? If not, what small changes can I begin to make?

2. If you are actively investing, keep on top of your finances. Set up a schedule for updating your portfolio, reading any material that's piled up, or furthering your education. Mark the "things you will do" on your calendar.

3. If you haven't started investing, here are three basic steps for getting started. Make a commitment to complete these three steps, writing down exactly what activities you will do on your calendar.

(1) Pay off your debts as quickly as possible.

(2) Every day (weekends included), put $1.50 plus all your spare change into a jar. At the end of the month, put the contents of the jar (it should be about $50) into a savings account.

(3) Set up an investment program. Select several mutual funds or individual stocks (perhaps with the help of an advisor). Either contact the fund company directly or set up an account with a brokerage firm. Contribute monthly by using dollar cost averaging.

4. If you're having difficulty doing anything at all, refer back to the checklist on page 174 ("Where do I Go Now?"), and follow the instructions. Do as much as you can, at a pace that feels comfortable. Remember, "Be not afraid of going slow, be only afraid of standing still."

• •

Realization #7:
I Can Make a Difference

It is by spending oneself that one becomes rich.
—SARAH BERNHARDT

Once, during an interview with Joseph Campbell on PBS several years ago, host Bill Moyers commented, "Unlike such heroes as Prometheus and Jesus, we're not going on our journeys to save the world but to save ourselves." To which Campbell responded, "By doing that you save the world." The aim of the hero's journey is not self-aggrandizement, Campbell insisted. "The ultimate aim is the wisdom and power to serve others."

It was this spirit beyond all else that inspired me, and in a way surprised me, during my interviews. I felt as if I were talking to true heroes while speaking to these women. Not just because they had become smart with money, bucking all kinds of emotional blocks, social taboos, and external obstacles. But because of what they did with their money once they got smart. I began to see that knowing how to invest wisely is merely the first part of taking responsibility. The other part, equally important, is recognizing one has the power to effect change.

Each woman told me, some with wide-eyed delight, how she came to the seventh realization, *"I can make a difference."* Each spoke of her desire to contribute to the world in a way that was also personally satisfying, typically through charitable donations, ethical investments, political contributions, businesses they started, or sometimes just by being able to help someone they loved.

"I always ran away from money before this," one woman said. "Then I realized I could use money to invest in companies I believed in, to support causes I believed in. It was like a rite of passage."

For a woman who may have once felt she needed to be rescued, this seventh realization—I can make a difference—simple as it sounds, can be a profound recognition, a momentous rite of passage. Once empowered, a woman becomes empowering, discovering within herself the wisdom and power to serve others.

Of course, if we're struggling with our own financial woes, the ills of the world will take second billing. I know this from experience. When I began my interviews years ago and someone mentioned a cause she supported or an issue she felt strongly about, I rarely pursued that line of questioning. All I wanted to know then was how these women managed their money. I didn't much care how they were using it. Only as I grew more financially adept did I become more interested in what they had to say about evoking change. Was this a coincidence? I don't think so. I was observing the process through my own progress.

Economic responsibility is an evolutionary phenomenon. As our financial life stabilizes, there is a natural progression from needing to get a grip on our money to wanting to extend our reach into the world. This was not something I expected to find when I started. I thought savvy investing was an end in itself. It was only after scores of interviews and personal conversations that I began to notice recurring comments like: "I have this urge to give back. That would be really pleasurable to me." This from a woman who had only recently started managing her money. Said another, "the fun is in the sharing."

I found statements like these to be a characteristic reaction upon the completion of the journey. As a woman feels financially secure and personally empowered, her thoughts begin to shift from "What do I have?" to "How much can I give?" As she stops waiting to be saved, she starts wanting to serve. As she figures out how to invest for the highest returns, she starts wondering where she can invest to achieve the most change. Money, a majority of women told me, provided them with time, flexibility, and the resources to focus on issues, shed light on specific problems, and figure out solutions.

Remember Anne Scheiber, the low-level government worker who amassed a fortune? Upon her death, she bequeathed her entire fortune to a college she never attended, Yeshiva University, to help disadvantaged Jewish women battle the kind of discrimination she felt she had encountered. According to a report in the *San Francisco Chronicle*: "As her fortune grew, so did her desire to make sure other women would not be shortchanged."

Not every single woman I interviewed said she wanted to change the world. Some indicated no interest in becoming good Samaritans, political activists, or social advocates. For them, the seventh realization was limited to activities like spending time with their family, pursuing a hobby, or seeing the world. This ability to make a difference at home or in one's personal life became reward enough. But my observation is that among the preponderance of women I interviewed, the seventh realization—I can make a difference—had a much broader scope and seemed to be the frequent offshoot of financial enlightenment.

Gwen, a former Silicon Valley executive who had earned "quite a bit of money" in the fledgling software industry, told me how it was for her. "As I became more sophisticated as an investor, I became more aware as a philanthropist," she said. "I believe philanthropy is an integral part of becoming smart with money. It's the next step." Gwen set up a foundation to fund women's causes, health care in particular. But she was quick to admit, "I absolutely had to learn about investing first. I wouldn't have any money left if I didn't." Then she added, "It can be learned. You don't have to have millions."

When I asked women like Gwen why they were doing what they did, their answers were essentially the same. "I saw money as something I could use to be more, do more, extend my scope, put my values into action," one woman told me.

"I don't know. Something just clicked," another said. "I realized I could have an impact with my money. I started focusing on where it went. I wanted to make sure my money wasn't detrimental to the earth and the people on it."

And another woman told me, "I always thought that something should be different in the world because I was there, something should be better. I wanted to do something worthwhile. I didn't want to be just a consumer. I wanted to bring my values alive. I just couldn't figure out how." What did she do? "I spent a year learning about money," she said. "I knew I didn't want to make a career out of investing, but I wanted to have enough money to do something in the world."

In the end, she helped fund a school for handicapped kids. "I value education," she told me, "and I felt strongly that disabled people deserve services." She hesitated for a moment, then said proudly, "There are a lot of kids in the world who are better off because of the work we did."

"I really believe that social change is possible," Marta Drury told me. Marta gives anywhere from one third to one half the income from her inheritance to women's and girls' programs. She also travels around the country, speaking on the importance of women's philanthropy. What makes Marta's story particularly inspiring is that she grew up in a working-class family, the daughter of a garbage collector. As a single parent, she raised her daughter on food stamps until she found work, where she earned, at best, $20,000 a year. Her father, meanwhile, sold his garbage business for millions and, when he died, left Marta his fortune. She was forty-six years old and had virtually no experience with money. She devoted six months to educating herself and has been using money to induce change ever since. "I saw my father go from poor to wealthy and the changes my own life has taken," Marta told me. "So I know change is possible, and I have the means to implement that."

These ordinary women were extraordinary role models for me. They motivated me to take responsibility for money, and they also inspired me to look beyond financial acumen as an end in itself. They became my models, not just as sharp investors, but as thoughtful, kind, and caring individuals who wanted to use their money in ways that mattered.

Philanthropy

I was especially struck by the creative and fulfilling ways women found to help others and the absolute joy they got from doing it. The women I interviewed were supporting cherished causes, or investing only in socially responsible companies, or starting businesses that reflected their passions, or electing female candidates to public office. Some women had major fortunes. The majority hadn't. Some were attempting ambitious projects. Most were doing very simple things. Some of their activities included grassroots social change. But many women were merely engaged in heartfelt acts of generosity to people they cared about. "Private philanthropy," Michal called it. For example, she gave her daughter, a burned-out social worker, enough money to take a year off from work and start a parenting center.

"I call that philanthropy," she said. "Look at what she did. She went out and created an organization. Although I wrote the check to my daughter, that was philanthropy."

Michal also created a Time Out Fund, which gives her adult children time away from their kids. Pamela puts a portion of her paycheck into a Kidnap Fund, which she dips into several times a year to surprise her husband with vacations. Another, who had inherited some money, bought her best friend a Jaguar for Christmas. "I knew she adored Jaguars," she told me. "She thought they were a work of art. And even if she won the lottery, she'd never buy one for herself."

Beyond their own family and friends, many women were reaching out into their communities. Some women actually devoted themselves full time to their philanthropy. These weren't just society matrons. Sandy, for example, had always worked in her family's bakery. When it was sold, she invested her share of the profits so she could live off the income from those investments, supplemented by occasional consulting jobs to small businesses. She didn't really know what she would do next.

One morning, while watching the *Today* show, she saw a program about a Seattle-based group, Community Voice Mail, that set up phone numbers through social service agencies to help homeless people find jobs. Inspired, she contacted the Seattle project and single-handedly started a similar program in San Francisco, doing all the fund raising, finding a sponsor, lining up discounted phone service. When that project was up and running, she put together another program, Working Essentials, which collects work-related items and personal-care products for homeless job hunters. Her philanthropy became her full-time profession, a consuming one at that.

Still, she admits, "There is a stigma about not being paid for work. It's not easy when someone says, 'What do you do?' But it's a choice I've made. Having money gives me this incredible opportunity." Interestingly, several women who either inherited or earned enough money to quit their salaried jobs expressed similar feelings of discomfort at not having what the world considers "a real job." Yet these women approached their charitable work, not as the diversion of "a Lady Bountiful" (as one woman put it), but as a serious career choice. One woman handed me her business card, which read, "Professional Philanthropist and Socially Responsible Investor."

Socially Responsible Investing

Philanthropy is one way to make a difference in the world. Investing is another. Many women I interviewed were using their investment dollars to facilitate change, investing not just for financial returns but to support companies that offer beneficial products and services, that support their employees and the community, and that take care of the environment. "Investing is like voting. It's our way of saying this is important to me," one woman asserted. And another asked me, "How could I be involved in things I don't believe in, that harm the world, and still sleep at night?"

"Twenty years ago, I was a nursery school teacher," Ellen, now a stockbroker, told me. "I saw my first article on Socially Responsible Investing in 1984. It's been a part of who I am ever since. It's a way you can put your values to work. You don't have to be invested in a company doing bad. You can put money into companies doing good, making people's lives better. It makes you feel like you have some control in how things are done. Our personal values don't have to go ignored."

I've heard the argument that Socially Responsible Investing is "pie in the sky," that it doesn't really make much difference, but not according to the women I spoke to. Amy Domini, a pioneer in the field of ethical investing, explained it this way: "If money is power, then it follows that the investing of money is the exercise of power. Shareholders are just beginning to realize their political power. The power is in our hands. All we have to do is use it."

"I have seen a lot of changes over the years. Look at South Africa," Marta told me, referring to the period between 1984 and 1990, when more than 200 companies withdrew at least part of their operations from South Africa, directly contributing to the end of apartheid. "That's a perfect example of what happens when large groups of people with money say *no*. It's slower in other areas, perhaps, but I feel it works. And at a personal level, knowing my money is invested sagely helps me live with myself." Marta, meanwhile, who has 100 percent of her investments in SRI, had a 27 percent return in 1995.

I also heard stories about women making money with innovative as well as compassionate projects. In my favorite story, a group of friends decided to pool their money and buy an apartment building that favored single mothers who were having trouble finding affordable housing. Each woman contributed enough to purchase a four-unit apartment building, and soon all four apartments were occupied by a single mother and her family. Eventually their group sold the four-unit building and bought a larger one. "We parlayed our profits into a bigger building and just kept selling up," this woman said. "We made excellent profits along with doing something worthwhile."

Starting Businesses

Others formed businesses as their way of contributing to causes they felt strongly about. When I interviewed Naomi, for example, she was in the process of selling the trucking company she founded and starting a women's venture fund to provide money, mentoring, and management training to women. "We're just in the early stages, but we're very committed and very excited," she told me.

"That's quite a big change for you," I said. "What happened?"

She answered immediately. "I wanted to make a difference," she said. "I asked myself, How do I take what I have, know, and love and make a difference?"

She knew that the biggest obstacle for women in business is capital. "They can't get it," she told me, and rattled off some figures: Forty percent of all businesses are held by women. These businesses account for the major growth in the net employment nationwide. And most of these women are primary breadwinners. Yet when women seek crucial financing, the money isn't there. Whether from banks, venture capitalists, or government agencies, less than 10 percent of all the available capital goes to these women. "Look at the impact on the community, employees, their children," Naomi declared. "If we don't start getting these women-owned businesses money, think about it. They're providing the jobs. Think about what will happen."

Small Contributions

Mother Teresa once said, "We can do no great things, only small things with great love." I heard many inspiring stories from women of average means who were doing just what they could afford, in areas they felt strongest about. Sherry, for example, told me how strongly she felt about supporting organizations like National Public Radio and the Center for Fairness and Action in the Media, which protects public dialogue and free speech. Even though she was involved in an expensive custody battle, she insisted that it was as important to budget for philanthropy as for her retirement account. "My whole philanthropic budget is $1,000 this year," she said. "My checks are small, $50 or $100. I'd love to do more, but I take what I do very seriously. And it makes me feel so good."

I met numerous women of like mind. "I'm not able to give huge amounts of money," one woman explained, "but when I see what people are doing to the environment, I want so much to effect change." She gives 5 percent of her teacher's salary to support environmental groups. And another told me: "Some people can write a check and not think. I am not in that position." But she does what she can. She was abused as a child, she told me; as an adult, she helps support a battered women's shelter. "I don't have an awful lot. I wish I had more. But what I do give is a reflection of who I am."

Giving as a reflection of who we are, no matter how small the amount, is a profoundly cogent statement of self-esteem and self-empowerment. These women declare, through their contributions, "I can make a difference in the problems that bother me most." Not only do they enhance their own self-image through doing, but they are improving the world around them.

Each Drop Makes a Difference

As I listened to these stories, I began to take a serious look at my own life. I had always considered myself generous. I gave money almost every time I was solicited. I've sent underprivileged kids to the circus and bought untold products from disabled veterans. I've dropped handfuls of change into Salvation Army buckets at Christmas and into those plastic boxes placed strategically on the supermarket checkout stand. I've made donations to all sorts of good causes, but nothing major, nothing I felt particularly keen about. Part of this was because, after the terrifying experience I went through with my tax bills, I had become timorous about parting with my money. But also, before these interviews, it never occurred to me that I should use my dollars to really make a difference in an area I felt passionate about. I think I figured that kind of giving was for other people, those far richer and more energetic than I.

I remember that in 1992, prompted by a persuasive friend, I wrote a fairly large check to Dianne Feinstein's U.S. senatorial campaign. In return, I was invited to a banquet for her supporters. I vividly recall looking around the jam-packed hall, feeling utterly insignificant. I felt my one check was nothing, just a drop in the bucket. I didn't think my contribution made any great difference; surely would never have been missed had I never given.

Then I interviewed Peggy, a self-employed political lobbyist who spoke fervently about the need to get women into political office. Peggy gave 32 percent of her salary to female candidates running for federal office, and that didn't include her other charitable donations.

"I am not wealthy," she told me bluntly. "No one who saw my income would call me wealthy. No way. But I've made some money, and I want to do something."

"But why do you give so much?" I asked.

"There's something about writing the check," she exclaimed. "For one thing, it makes me feel so good I can't tell you. And second, I know it's important. I know my check makes a difference."

"Really? I've never felt like that," I admitted. "I give to charity, but I've never felt that my little check made much of a difference at all."

"A lot of women feel like that," Peggy said. "They need to be educated on how their small checks make a difference. They need to see how they effect change. Barbara Boxer's [successful 1992 U.S. senatorial] campaign was funded almost totally by small checks. It's all those little checks that make the difference."

And this does not apply just to politics, she asserted. Peggy had also created two $500 college scholarships for disadvantaged minorities in her old high school. "Five hundred dollars might not sound like much," she declared, "but I know it can make a big difference to those kids."

Did other women feel the same? "How do you keep from feeling your contributions are just a drop in the bucket?" I asked the women I interviewed. "I *am* just a drop in the bucket," Naomi replied, "but all those little drops fill the bucket."

Not every woman answered so forcefully. When I asked Sandy, who works with the homeless, whether she believes her efforts really make a difference, tears came to her eyes. "It can be almost overwhelming," she replied. "Sometimes I know I'm making a difference. Sometimes I don't. But I still keep on giving."

I heard something similar from Linda Pei when she explained why she started the Women's Equity Mutual Fund, which invests only in companies that support their female employees and women's issues. "I felt I had to do something I felt passionate about," she said. "Not just for the paycheck but for a higher purpose." She tells me the story of how the idea for the fund came about. She had been talking to a friend about the problems women were having getting ahead in the workplace and recalled saying, "Somebody should do something about this." The two women looked at each other and realized that if everyone said the same thing, nothing would happen. After much thought and painstaking research, the two decided to create a mutual fund with a dual goal: to empower women financially and to impel companies to pay attention to women's issues.

"Sometimes," Linda says, "I wake up in the middle of the night, panicked. I don't want to be another example of a woman failing." Yet, she says, "I believe in this. I may not be able to change the world, but I can do my little part."

The more women I talked to, the more I heard comments like Linda's. I began to understand that it takes courage to carry out the seventh realization, to attempt to make a difference.

"There are times I've been terrified about money," said Sherry, who is the director of a nonprofit women's organization. "Still, though I may not be able to buy clothes for myself, I will write a check to the public radio station or the Center for Constitutional Law."

Even those with large fortunes reported similar moments of fear over money. "Sure I get scared sometimes," Marta admitted during our interview. "I know how hard my family worked for it, all the sacrifices we made. I feel very responsible for this money." And when the government took one third right off the bat, she said, "I saw how quickly it can go. But I also felt it was this enormous cosmic gift I wanted to share."

The Art of Giving

Just as these women were courageous in their sharing, they were methodical in their approach. I was fascinated to learn that most of the women I interviewed gave as much thought to their charitable donations as they did their investment dollars.

A well-known philanthropist, Tracy Gary, told me, "I had all these groups coming and asking me for money. I saw that I was giving to those groups that had the best sales pitch." She pulled back and made a plan. "A plan gives you a reason to say yes and a reason to say no."

"How do you make a plan?" I asked.

"Start with your own concerns, your own vision. Be reflective," Tracy advised. "Choose a few areas to finance, ones connected with your passion."

That's precisely what the women I interviewed told me they had done. They took a long, hard look at what they cared most about, what mattered to them, what really made them feel good. It was not always an easy task. Many were struggling to identify their values, asking themselves: What is the best use of my money, time, and energy? Where can I really make a difference?

Michal told me about a powerful group exercise she once participated in. "We got out our receipts for the previous two years and broke them into categories of giving: education, environment, politics, health, and so forth. Then we asked ourselves: Did my giving reflect my priorities? Was I doing what I wanted? Would I like to be doing it differently? One woman saw that 90 percent of her charitable money was going to her church. She loved her church, but she wanted to do more." Michal, who is seventy, also made adjustments. "My priorities had changed," she explained. "I never gave to the Older Women's League before. Nor did I ever support women's candidates—there weren't any to give to."

"The art of giving is very hard," a real estate agent told me. "There are a zillion organizations. You have to decide who you want to help and how. I like to help people who have no way to help themselves, like children. I also love opera and used to sing opera." So she had recently donated her car to a children's center and had given a large sum to the opera guild.

"How did you decide how much you would give?" I started asking women. Practically all of them worked up a budget. Before they gave a penny, these women told me, they figured out how much they had and how much they could give, treating philanthropy as one of their expenses. Marta, for example, meets with her advisor several times a year. "He keeps me sober." She laughed. "This year I built a house, so I really dipped into my capital." But rather than cut her philanthropy budget, Marta reduced her personal budget.

"Having a budget really helps, doesn't it?" I said. Her eyes lit up. "I love having a budget!" she exclaimed. "It helps me feel in control. I budget my philanthropy out about a year in advance. I know how much I have. I know how much I need to make. I know how much I can afford to give away."

Many women set up separate philanthropic accounts, sometimes with their spouses, sometimes not. One woman told me she'd been brought up in a philanthropic family but her husband hadn't. "In order to feel okay about giving," she said, "I always had a separate account for it. It was important to me." And Marta not only had a special investment portfolio earmarked for philanthropy; she also put $2,000 each year in a philan- thropic account to get her teenage daughter used to making charitable contributions and, says Marta, "to experience what my work is about, a form of 'take your daughter to work.'"

Many others leveraged their giving, in exchange for seats on the board, stipulating that their interests and values be expressed, or requiring matching grants in return for their donations, as Gwen's foundation does. "I'm trying to influence other women to make gifts and change institu- tions, to leverage my wealth by getting other people to join me," she told me. "We can have far greater impact that way." Then she added some- thing particularly significant. "If you look at history, change occurs in small increments. A lot of people making small changes can have transfor- mative results."

The Corollary

Women like Marta, Sandy, and Gwen were as much examples of be- nevolence as they were models of power. From them I discovered that there is a corollary to the seventh realization, and it goes like this: *Indi- vidually, I can make a difference; together, we can make an even bigger difference.* And herein lies the true power. Women are just begin- ning to recognize that our individual checks, combined with others, be it a charitable donation, a political contribution, or an ethical investment, create widespread social change.

Gwen told me about an experience she had when she attended a con- ference on philanthropy with a small group of women. "I looked around the room and saw what a powerful force women could be if we used our money for social change," she exclaimed. "Just the sheer numbers!" Gwen's insight is not only personally perceptive but potentially staggering in terms of its impact.

"I always felt the problems of the world were so big. Who was I to try to solve any of them? I'd get so paralyzed," Linda Pei told me. "What I didn't realize is what happens when people pull together, how much power we have. I started the mutual fund with the idea that collectively we can make a big difference. It doesn't matter how much money we have individually. Collectively we have power."

Indeed, women are coming together in informal groups and organized coalitions, accomplishing more in unison than they ever could by themselves. I was amazed at the number of organizations devoted to helping women that are sprouting up all over the country: the Women Donors Network, The Women's Funding Exchange, The Committee of 200, Emily's List, The International Women's Forum, The Women's Economic Development Center. It is a list that could fill pages. Such alliances are becoming potent catalysts for social change.

"We have to aggregate power," declared Judith Luther-Wilder, founder of one such group, Women, Inc., a non-profit organization that helps its members secure business loans. "Women have to join together in the same way senior citizens have through AARP. We have enormous clout if we use it."

More and more, women are joining together, wielding their clout. Let us not underestimate the significance of this occurrence. I believe a quiet but profound revolution is underway, a revolution quiet enough to go almost unnoticed but profound enough to have extraordinary impact. As more women learn to use their money consciously and responsibly, they are virtually reshaping the world—socially, economically, and politically.

New York Times columnist Anthony Lewis wrote of this phenomenon in 1992, "There is a profound change in American politics and culture. Women: they are the change. . . . Women are demonstrating their power in the way politicians understand best—with money."

The authors of *Megatrends for Women* concur. "When the subject is women, what is happening is awesome," they write. "Millions of women the world over are taking economic and political power, building new institutions, infusing them with new, more humanistic values, saving the world or part of it."

Imagine if a critical mass of women were to become economically independent and financially responsible. "You could almost cure the ills of the world if more women were financially empowered," one woman declared. "We are a force to be reckoned with," another proclaimed proudly.

Ironically, the very traits that have kept women locked in traditional roles—caring, compassion, sensitivity, nurturing—are the same traits that, once we're empowered, become the thrust of our effectiveness. It's not so far-fetched that women, who have always been the caretakers and homemakers, would have the vision and values to heal our planet, our home. But it takes more than high ideals, glorious visions, and feminine values to cure the world's ills. It takes money.

"Philanthropy is the final frontier for women," said Sondra Shaw, co-director of the National Network on Women as Philanthropists. I thought it a curious statement. Women have always volunteered for social causes. But it has been time, rarely money, that they gave, she pointed out.

Still today, though 90 percent of charitable donations come from individuals, women give far less than men. One study found that men donate 3.8 percent of their income, while women only give 1.8 percent. The reasons for this discrepancy vary. Some women have relied on their husbands to make donations for both of them. Others see philanthropy as frivolous when there are more important things to spend money on. Some women don't feel their small check can make a difference. And of course, we have no role models for this kind of giving among women, nor were we socialized to connect giving with power. Besides, women earn less than men and therefore may be afraid to jeopardize their finances. "If you're not used to writing checks, it hurts," said Peggy. "But once you get used to it"—she winked—"it hurts less."

When women do give, studies show that their priorities reflect their life experiences as they differ from men's. No surprise to anyone, women are more concerned with social issues, health care, and domestic problems. They are less likely to support large mainstream agencies, and more interested in new and different causes where they believe their gift will make a difference and they can play a role.

For a perfect example, in the year after the 1992 election, which sent an unprecedented fourteen women to Congress, the House and Senate approved a record sixty-six bills focusing on women's issues, everything from research into breast cancer to recruiting more women science teachers.

"This whole idea of women supporting women with their money is fairly new," Gloria Steinem says. "It's just as revolutionary as votes for women." And just as potent.

Tracy Gary is an inspiring example. While working at a battered-women's shelter, she noticed a document lying on top of a stack of mail—a report on charitable donations. Only one percent of all charitable dollars, she read, was used to fund programs for women and girls. The major funding sources, like United Way, which raised millions of dollars annually, all but ignored battered women, low-income mothers, and other women's causes. At the same time, more and more women were sinking deeper into poverty.

Tracy could not ignore this appalling unfairness. In 1979, with a handful of other women, she founded the San Francisco Women's Foundation, the first community foundation in the country to fund local women's programs. Tracy knew that no matter how much money a woman had in the bank, she wouldn't give if she was insecure, anxious, or ignorant. But Tracy was equally convinced that once enough women became knowledgeable and financially secure, and took control of their money, they would have the resources, sensitivity, and values to be able to change the world. To that end, she founded Resourceful Women, a nonprofit organization for financial education.

"I've seen what happens when women blossom into their full potential," she told me. "Their families are so much stronger. Their communities are stronger. The world is stronger."

Tracy recalled a story she once heard at a conference on women and power. "The speaker told of a song that women in Africa sing when they are working together. The only lyrics are: 'Lift while you climb.' To me, that's very much what our power can do. As you stretch for yourself to get to where you want to go, always have a hand stretched down to help someone.

"As you learn, if you will pass on what you've learned to someone who doesn't know as much or have as many resources, then you're really bettering the world." But she insists, "We have got to stop thinking someone else will change the world. We've got to get that we're the ones."

Because of women like Tracy, Linda, Marta, Peggy, Sandy, Sherry, Michal, and thousands of others, there are more than seventy-five foundations raising tens of millions of dollars exclusively for women's programs, compared with only a handful a decade ago. Over 50 percent of the money flowing into socially responsible mutual funds comes from women. Emily's

List, which raised an unparalleled $15 million for pro-choice Democratic women candidates in the 1992 election, has become the largest political action committee in the United States. And even though government funding is drying up, there are public radio stations still broadcasting, homeless people finding jobs, battered women who have somewhere to go, and handicapped kids with a place to learn.

This is what happens when women tap their tremendous potential. Perhaps a poster in Tracy's office says it best: "Never doubt that a small group of thoughtful committed citizens can change the world. Indeed, it's the only thing that ever has."

It's Just the Beginning

> *"Become the change you want to make."*
> —MAHATMA GANDHI

We have come to the end of a journey that never really ends—financial responsibility is an ongoing endeavor. Along the way, however, we've discovered a surprising truth. The illusory prince is but our own potential, waiting to be developed. We've found within *us* the authority we once sought without. No longer passive princesses, we've become responsible adults. The realizations have been our awakening. Our future is full of promise. Achieving economic independence is truly a personal triumph, a cause for celebration, a gift to the world as well as ourselves. Now let us spread our wings, reclaim our power, and celebrate our progress. It is our time to fly.

••• CHAPTER TEN RECAPPED •••

Realization—Something happens when a woman becomes financially responsible. She becomes powerful. She has the means to effect change, to really make a difference, in areas of life that matter to her most. And when an economically independent woman joins with other smart women, they wield tremendous social, economical, and political clout. Together, women can become the driving force that will actually transform the world and ultimately heal the planet.

(These "To Do's" are, of course, optional. They are not necessary for becoming smart, or even wise. But if you seek to make the world a better place, to give of yourself in ways that matter, then these are some suggestions.)

To Do

1. Find out more about *Resourceful Women* and *The Women's Donor Network* (Resourceful Women, Presidio Building 1016, P.O. Box 29423, San Francisco, CA 94129-0423). Also, the *Impact Project* (21 Linwood St., Arlington, MA 02174). Both are a wealth of resources.

2. Read *Investing from the Heart: The Guide to Socially Responsible Investing,* by Jack A. Brill and Alan Reder (Crown Publishers), and *We Gave Away a Fortune,* by Christopher Mogil and Anne Slepian (New Society Publishers). Both books are interesting reading. The first one is educational, the latter inspirational. Also, ask for a free copy of *Giving Wisely, Giving Well—A Consumer Guide to Charitable Giving* from Fidelity Investments Charitable Services (800-258-5759).

3. Ask yourself: Where would I like to see change? What social problem(s) gives me the greatest concern? How would I most like to make a difference in my family/neighborhood/community/world? Give these questions some thought. Then mull this over: What is one thing I could do personally to make a difference? Are there any organizations I could support that are effecting change? Then make a contribution, in time or money, no matter how small.

Appendix

• •

RESOURCE GUIDE

This is by no means a definitive list. These are simply the resources I found the most helpful, or were suggested by experts I trusted or most often mentioned by the women I interviewed.

Internet

Visit my Web site at http://www.princequiz.com. At this site you can take the quiz "Where Are You When It Comes to Money?" and it will be scored for you. You can also link up to all kinds of other financial Web sites.

Publications

These are, in my opinion, the best financial journals currently on the market:

- *Smart Money* (800-444-4204)
- *Kiplinger's Personal Finance Magazine* (800-544-0155)
- *Wall Street Journal* (800-JOURNAL)
- *New York Times,* Sunday business section
- *Worth Magazine* (800–777–1851)

Freebies

The following companies, which offer a variety of investment services, are wonderful resources for learning about *financial planning, investing,* and *retirement.* Call and find out what they offer, especially in the way of free educational brochures, booklets, and seminars. (This is a very limited list. As you read financial publications, you'll notice all kinds of ads for free material. I urge you to send for any that sound interesting.)

- *T. Rowe Price* (800-638-5660)
- *Fidelity* (800-544-8888)
- *Scudder, Stevens, & Clark* (800-225-2470)
- *American Express Financial Advisors* (800-437-3500)
- *Charles Schwab* (800-435-4000)
- *The Vanguard Group* (800-662-7447)
- *American Association of Retired Persons* (800-424-3410)
- *Oppenheimer Management Corp.* (800-456-1699)

Investing

- *How to Buy Stocks* by Louis Engel. Columnist Herb Greenberg said, "If I could buy just one book, it would be this."
- *Making the Most of Your Money: Smart Ways to Create Wealth and Plan Your Finances in the 90s,* by Jane Bryant Quinn (Harper-Business, 1994), and *Terry Savage's New Money Strategies for the '90s,* by Terry Savage (Simon & Schuster, 1991). These books will tell you just about everything you need to know concerning money and investing. They are wonderful reference books, but they can be a bit overwhelming for the beginner.
- *The Wall Street Journal Guide to Understanding Personal Finance.* Dow Jones & Co., Inc., P.O. Box 300, Princeton, NJ 08543-0300. This slim, easy-to-read booklet uses lots of colorful graphics to teach you the financial basics. (Also available from same address: *Barron's Video Guide to Mutual Funds.*)
- *Money Smart: Secrets Women Need to Know About Money,* by Esther Berger (Simon & Schuster, 1993). Stockbroker Esther Berger writes with a sense of humor and a genuine desire to cut through the "broker-speak" so many of her colleagues engage in.
- *Personal Finance for Dummies,* by Eric Tyson (IDG Books, 1994). The author, an accomplished financial writer, takes an enormous amount of material, organizes it concisely, adds whimsical icons and cute cartoons, and then makes it great fun to read.

- *One Up on Wall Street* and *Beating the Street*, by Peter Lynch (Simon & Schuster, 1989, 1993). These national best-sellers are immensely readable and very motivational. The legendary Lynch will truly have you believing that any novice can become a successful investor. The whole time I was reading *One Up on Wall Street*, Lynch's first book, I kept thinking, I can do this!

Newsletters

- *Morningstar Five Star Investor* (800-876-5005), $79 a year. If you only subscribe to one newsletter for mutual funds, this is it. I find it extremely instructive.
- *Hulbert's Financial Digest*, by Mark Hulbert (888–485–2378), $59 a year. This is the newsletter to check before subscribing to any others. Hulbert tracks and rates the performance of other newsletter writers. Look for *Hulbert's* in the library or call for a sample copy. (In fact, when ordering any newsletter, ask for a sample copy.)

Couples

If you have a spouse, "significant other," or are even thinking about the possibility, these books will make a big difference in your joint financial life.

- *What Every Woman Should Know About Her Husband's Money*, by Shelby White (Random House, 1992, 1995).
- *Couples and Money*, by Victoria Felton-Collins (Bantam Books, 1990).

Psychology

- *Unbalanced Accounts: How Women Can Overcome Their Fear of Money*, by Annette Lieberman and Vicki Lindner (Penguin Books, 1987). This anecdotal guide explores the "moneyphobia" that plagues women and tells how many have overcome their fear of managing money.
- *Warm Hearts and Cold Cash: The Intimate Dynamics of Families and Money*, by Marcia Millman (Free Press, 1991). If you want insight into how your family has affected your feelings about money, this is the book to read.
- *Money Is My Friend*, by Phil Laut (Trinity Publications, 1978). This

classic how-to book is full of techniques for changing your self-image and the way you think about money. I loved it!

Investment Clubs

- *National Association of Investors Corporation*, P.O. Box 220, Royal Oak, MI 48068. In addition to information about investment clubs, NAIC publishes a very good financial magazine, *Better Investing*, and it is also an excellent source for Dividend Reinvestment Plans. Check them out!
- *Starting and Running a Profitable Investment Club: The Official Guide from the National Association of Investment Clubs*, by Thomas E. O'Hara and Kenneth S. Janke, Sr. (Random House, 1996). If you want to start an investment club, this is really the only book you need. My mother, who just formed one, swears by it!

Organizations

- *Resourceful Women*. A genuinely helpful nonprofit group whose sole purpose is to educate and support women with wealth. Their definition of wealth: anyone who has assets over inherited or earned $25,000. Presidio Building 1016, P.O. Box 29423, San Francisco, CA 94129-0423.
- *Women Donors Network*. A national network for women who annually donate more than $25,000 to philanthropies. They offer a variety of stimulating programs and an engaging newletter. Presidio Building 1016, P.O. Box 29423, San Francisco, CA 94129-0423.
- *American Association of Individual Investors, Inc.* 625 N. Michigan Ave., Chicago, IL 60611 (312-280-0170). AAII offers very good financial seminars, taught by exceptionally qualified personnel, all over the country. They also have regional meetings with some notable speakers. I highly recommend their gatherings for both beginning and experienced investors.
- *National Center for Women and Retirement Research*. This university-based nonprofit center does extensive research on women's financial needs. They also publish books and tapes, and offer seminars on financial skills. Sign up for their newsletter (800-426-7386).

Socially Responsible Investing

- *Ethical Investing: How to Make Profitable Investments Without Sacrificing Your Principles*, by Amy Domini (Addison Wesley, 1984). Domini is a pioneer in the field.

- *Investing with Your Conscience: How to Achieve High Returns Using Socially Responsible Investing,* by John Harrington (John Wiley, 1992).

Philanthropy

- *We Gave Away a Fortune,* by Christopher Mogil and Anne Slepian. This is a compendium of very compelling stories about people who gave away significant portions of their wealth to make the world better. Impact Project, 2244 Alder St., Eugene, OR 97405.
- *The National Network on Women as Philanthropists.* This network for encouraging women's philanthropy publishes a quarterly newsletter, "Women's Philanthropy," that's both inspiring and informative. 1300 Linden Drive, Madison, WI 53706-1575 (608-262-1962).
- *The Impact Project.* I highly recommend checking out this unique and wonderful nonprofit educational group that is truly committed to philanthropy. They offer publications, support groups, workshops, and counseling. 21 Linwood St., Arlington, MA 02174 (617-648-0776).
- *Charitable Giving: A Tax Guide for Individual Donors.* Arthur Andersen & Co. (800-546-3209). This informative guide to getting tax benefits for your charitable donations doesn't get bogged down in technicalities.

Inherited Wealth

- *The Legacy of Inherited Wealth: Interviews with Heirs,* by Barbara Blouin, Katherine Gibson, and Margaret Kiersted. Inheritors talk about their experiences with inheriting money. Anyone in this situation, or who expects to be, will find these personal stories very moving. Inheritance Project, 3291 Deer Run Road, Blacksburg, VA 94060.
- *More Than Money.* An inspiring and entertaining quarterly newsletter written by and for people with wealth. It's always full of fascinating stories. Impact Project, 2244 Alder St., Eugene, OR 97405.

Debt and Bankruptcy

- *National Center for Financial Education.* A nonprofit educational organization dedicated to helping people do a better job of spending, saving, planning, investing, and insuring for their financial future. P.O. Box 34070, San Diego, CA 92163 (619-232-8811).

- *Debtors Anonymous*. Modeled after Alcoholics Anonymous, DA provides support for breaking spending and debting habits. Check your local phone directory or write DA, P.O. Box 400, Grand Central Station, New York, NY 10163-0400.
- *Financial Recovery Workbook*. Financial Recovery Center, 40 Sir Francis Drake Blvd., San Anselmo, CA 94960 (800-722-0110). Created by a pioneer in the field of financial recovery, this excellent workbook offers worksheets, written exercises, and solid advice for controlling spending and eliminating debt without going into a life of deprivation.
- *Overcoming Overspending: A Winning Plan for Spenders and Their Partners*, by Olivia Mellan (Walker & Company, 1997). The author is a noted psychotherapist specializing in money issues. She's a wonderful writer and offers so many helpful ways to eliminate debt. It's the first book I've seen that also helps you deal with a loved one who overspends.

Financial Professionals

- To check out a stockbroker's background, call the *National Association of Security Dealers* (800-289-9999).
- For financial planners, contact:

    Institute of Certified Financial Planners (800-282-7526). They'll send you, free, three names of financial planners in your area who have been licensed by the ICFP. They'll include a brochure on selecting an advisor, with questions to ask.

    National Association of Personal Financial Advisors (800-366-2732). They'll send you a free list of fee-only financial planners in your area, along with a brochure about finding and using professional advisors.

    American Institute of Certified Public Accountants' Personal Financial Planning Division (800-862-4272). They will send you a national listing of CPAs, organized by states and cities, who are personal financial specialists, plus two educational brochures.

- *Investor Protection Trust*. For a free brochure on how to prevent and resolve conflicts with advisors, write IPF, 1901 North Fort Myer Drive, Suite 1012, Arlington, VA 22209.

Notes

●●●●●●●●●●●●●●●●●●●●●●●●●●●

p. 24: *The Wall Street Journal*, June 11, 1992.

p. 25: *Ms.* magazine, November 1989.

Forbes magazine, October 21, 1991.

p. 28: *Self* magazine, January 1988.

The Los Angeles Times, December 20, 1994.

p. 47: *The New York Times*, July 1, 1990 (both citations).

p. 48: *Working Woman* magazine, September 1995 (both citations).

p. 87: *Worth* magazine, June 1993.

p. 104: *International Herald Tribune*, January 1, 1996.

p. 105: *Fortune* magazine, October 31, 1995. Cover story: "The Coming Investment Revolt."

p. 106: *Smart Money Moves for the '90s* by the editors of *Money* magazine. Time, Inc., 1990.

Herb Greenberg in *The San Francisco Chronicle*, October 31, 1995.

p. 133: *The International Herald Tribune*, December 30-31, 1995; January 1, 1996.

Louis Rukeyser's Mutual Funds. Newsletter, July 1994.

p. 149: *Financial Planning* magazine, September 1989.

Family Therapy Networker: Article reprinted in *Utne Reader*, September/October 1992.

Index

FOR THE BEST IN PAPERBACKS, LOOK FOR THE

In every corner of the world, on every subject under the sun, Penguin represents quality and variety—the very best in publishing today.

For complete information about books available from Penguin—including Puffins, Penguin Classics, and Arkana—and how to order them, write to us at the appropriate address below. Please note that for copyright reasons the selection of books varies from country to country.

In the United Kingdom: Please write to *Dept. JC, Penguin Books Ltd, FREEPOST, West Drayton, Middlesex UB7 0BR.*

If you have any difficulty in obtaining a title, please send your order with the correct money, plus ten percent for postage and packaging, to *P.O. Box No. 11, West Drayton, Middlesex UB7 0BR*

In the United States: Please write to *Consumer Sales, Penguin USA, P.O. Box 999, Dept. 17109, Bergenfield, New Jersey 07621-0120.* VISA and MasterCard holders call 1-800-253-6476 to order all Penguin titles

In Canada: Please write to *Penguin Books Canada Ltd, 10 Alcorn Avenue, Suite 300, Toronto, Ontario M4V 3B2*

In Australia: Please write to *Penguin Books Australia Ltd, P.O. Box 257, Ringwood, Victoria 3134*

In New Zealand: Please write to *Penguin Books (NZ) Ltd, Private Bag 102902, North Shore Mail Centre, Auckland 10*

In India: Please write to *Penguin Books India Pvt Ltd, 706 Eros Apartments, 56 Nehru Place, New Delhi 110 019*

In the Netherlands: Please write to *Penguin Books Netherlands bv, Postbus 3507, NL-1001 AH Amsterdam*

In Germany: Please write to *Penguin Books Deutschland GmbH, Metzlerstrasse 26, 60594 Frankfurt am Main*

In Spain: Please write to *Penguin Books S. A., Bravo Murillo 19, 1° B, 28015 Madrid*

In Italy: Please write to *Penguin Italia s.r.l., Via Felice Casati 20, I-20124 Milano*

In France: Please write to *Penguin France S. A., 17 rue Lejeune, F–31000 Toulouse*

In Japan: Please write to *Penguin Books Japan, Ishikiribashi Building, 2–5–4, Suido, Bunkyo-ku, Tokyo 112*

In Greece: Please write to *Penguin Hellas Ltd, Dimocritou 3, GR–106 71 Athens*

In South Africa: Please write to *Longman Penguin Southern Africa (Pty) Ltd, Private Bag X08, Bertsham 2013*